Praise for this book

'A very nice job! And the details of your book gave me a much
better idea of life in the nineteenth century in England.... In
addition, I find your style pleasing – fluid and with a brisk
pace.' — Barry Tharaud, editor of *Nineteenth-Century Prose*

'A staggering piece of research'
— Laurence Bristow-Smith (researcher and writer)

Harriet Martineau,

Miss J, and Ellen McKee

G. Peter Winnington

☙

The Letterworth Press

Published in Switzerland by the Letterworth Press
https://TheLetterworthPress.org
Third edition

Whilst every care has been taken to ensure the accuracy of the
information in this monograph, the publisher cannot accept
responsibility for any mistakes that may have been included.
Persons wishing to supply corrections or additional information,
of any kind, are invited to contact the author.

ISBN 978-2-9701307-0-3

1 3 5 7 9 8 6 4 2

A Note on the Third Edition

When this monograph was first published, the original typeface proved to be ill-matched to the subject matter. Setting the text in a different font caused a few changes in the page breaks; I took the opportunity to correct one or two verbal infelicities. So that was the second edition.

Some time later, I learned that on Harriet Martineau's death, her copy of William Henry Bartlett's *American Scenery*, published in 1840, was given to Miss J by HM's relatives as a memento. Looking at the illustrations, I discovered a view of the newly opened railway line at Little Falls, roughly half way between Boston and Buffalo (both of which HM and Miss J visited when they first arrived in America). I had long wanted to see what the carriages they travelled in – and the locomotives that pulled the trains – had looked like in the mid-1830s, but had been unable to find any usable pictures of them. This picture, showing an engine closely resembling Stephenson's famous Locomotion No 1 (1825) rather than the Stourbridge Lion (1828) which was purchased by the Delaware and Hudson Canal Company, answered my desire. So I have placed it on page 37.

At the same time, I removed a paragraph about a letter that I had previously taken to refer to Miss J, but which turned out to be about her aunt Louisa Perina Courtauld (II). So the pagination changed again.

These improvements make this the third edition.   GPW

Our actions are like ships which we may watch sail out to sea, and not know when or with what cargo they will return to port. —Iris Murdoch in *The Bell*

At THE AGE OF THIRTY, Harriet Martineau (1802–76) sprang to instant fame – first national, and then international – with a series of novellas entitled *Illustrations of Political Economy*. At the time, the science of political economy was the exclusive province of male theoreticians like Adam Smith (1723–90), whose *Wealth of Nations* in 1776 described the free market economy, Robert Malthus* (1766–1834), whose views on population growth remain controversial, and David Ricardo (1772–1823), who worked out *Principles of Political Economy and Taxation* (1817).

No one – not even Martineau's own mother – could imagine that a young woman might be able to get her mind around these concepts, still less write credible stories about how they worked in practice. Typical was the leading political economist of the day, James Mill; he sneered that 'if the young lady must try her hand at Political Economy, she should write it in the orthodox didactic style.'[1] Yet each of Martineau's very readable stories, which were published at monthly intervals over a period of two years, set one of the principles of political economy in a context of everyday life, making them accessible to everyone. And everyone bought them. With sales reaching ten thousand copies a month, they rivalled in popularity the serialized novels that were shortly to come from Charles Dickens.

Politicians were quick to make use of this new pen: the Chancellor, Lord Brougham, requested a series of *Illustrations*

---

* After Martineau became famous, she met Malthus and enjoyed his conversation.

of Taxation and then, in preparation for the New Poor Law that was passed in August 1834, he asked for a further series, *Poor Laws and Paupers Illustrated*. HM (the abbreviation I shall use from now on for Harriet Martineau) wrote them for him at once, while still continuing to produce a fresh *Illustration* story every month. At that point, James Mill 'made the frankest possible acknowledgment [to HM] of his mistake in saying that political economy could not be conveyed in fiction, and that the public would not receive it in any but the didactic form.'[2]

Although politicians sought out HM for her advice, she was by no means a popular figure. She was too intelligent and – confident in the logic of her arguments – she expressed herself too vigorously. Women were not expected to have opinions, and certainly not to voice them in public. Because such outspokenness was socially unacceptable, women were embarrassed by her. As for men, when HM declined a state pension because she feared that she would lose her independence by it, Lord Brougham exploded: 'I hate a woman who has opinions. She has refused a pension, – making herself out to be better than other people.'[3] She remained controversial throughout her life.

HM's wide learning was gained largely through self-education. Few girls were schooled beyond the three Rs; then they were set to household tasks. Yet as early as February 1823, using the male pseudonym 'Discipulus' and writing as though she were a man, HM had argued (in the *Monthly Repository*) in favour of equal educational opportunities for girls and boys. To anyone else, the idea that women might be capable of benefitting from higher education was unimaginable. In the 1830s, 'the universities had not even contemplated the possibility of Fellows having wives; they were horrified fifty years later at the mere suggestion of girl graduates.'[4] So when HM revealed her exceptional intelligence and learning by invading the man's world of political economy, she passed for a freak. Feeling threatened, men disparaged her.

George Eliot might almost have had HM in mind when she had Mr Tulliver declare, in *The Mill on Floss,* that 'an over-'cute [i.e. very clever] woman's no better nor a long-tailed sheep, – she'll fetch none the bigger price [on the marriage market] for that.' Once HM became famous, only one man ever expressed any romantic interest in her (so far as we know), and that was Charles Darwin's brother Erasmus. But he soon realized that he was intellectually outclassed. 'Our only protection from so admirable a sister-in-law,' wrote Charles,

> is in her working him too hard. He begins to perceive, (to use his own expression) he shall be not much better than her 'nigger' [i.e. slave]. – Imagine poor Erasmus a nigger to so philosophical and energetic a lady.... She already takes him to task about his idleness – She is going some day to explain to him her notions about marriage – Perfect equality of rights is part of her doctrine. I much doubt whether it will be equality in practice. We must pray for our poor 'nigger'.[5]

His prayers were answered: after a couple of years of going out and dining together, HM and Erasmus Darwin drifted apart; he remained a bachelor. HM was indeed 'over-'cute', a unique phenomenon. As Mr Tulliver complained, 'That's the worst on't wi' crossing o' breeds: you can never justly calkilate what'll come on't.'[6]

In her stories, HM revealed her democratic views with limpid clarity, which made her unpopular with heads of state too. In France, Louis Philippe placed a large order for copies of the *Illustrations* and commanded that they be translated and distributed to schools throughout the country. Then he read the story called 'French Wines and Politics', which HM set during the French Revolution – and back-pedalled frantically, cancelling those plans. Another story, 'The Charmed Sea', featuring Poles who had been exiled to Siberia, similarly incensed the Tsar, who until that point had been full of admiration for the *Illustrations*: he ordered every copy in Russia to be burned, and

declared HM *persona non grata*. Austria, where a German trans-
lation was in hand, followed suit. To Mrs Marcet,* who pointed
out to her the offence she was causing, HM retorted that she
'wrote with a view to the people, and especially the most suffer-
ing of them; and the crowned heads must for once take their
chance for their feelings.'[7]

'I knew I was right,' she wrote, 'and people who are aware that
they are in the right need never lose [their] temper.' She knew
that 'people wanted the *Illustrations*' and so she was resolved that
they should have them, even though 'the effort would probably
be fatal to my reputation.'[8] Her fears were well founded; her
reputation has indeed never recovered.

Of the heads of state who read her stories, only the young
Princess Victoria remained unchanging in her admiration for
HM; *Illustrations of Political Economy* were among her favourite
story books; she was heard to exclaim with delight at seeing
an advertisement for the *Taxation* series. She invited HM to
her coronation – and HM wrote derisively about the ancient
customs (and people) that she saw at the ceremony.

By July 1834, HM was – understandably – exhausted by so
much writing. At this point she decided to take the rest that she
had been promising herself. In her *Autobiography*, she spelled
out what a *rest* meant for her; she aimed to

> break through any selfish 'particularity' that might be growing
> on me with years, and any love of ease and indulgence that
> might have arisen out of success, flattery, or the devoted kind-
> ness of my friends. I believed that it would be good for me to
> 'rough it' for a while, before I grew too old and fixed in my
> habits for such an experiment.[9]

She was a woman who 'truly lived instead of vegetated.'[10] Her
words remind me of what Captain Scott wrote to his wife, on the

---

* Jane Marcet (1769–1858) was a major popularizer of chemistry; she also
wrote a volume of *Conversations on Political Economy* (1816), intended
for schoolgirls, which inspired HM when she read it in 1827.

day he died after reaching the South Pole: 'How much better has it been than lounging in too great comfort at home.'[11] They reveal the drive and determination that make HM such a unique figure. Instead of heading for the Continent, like everyone else, she decided on a two-year visit to the largely undeveloped country of America, where she would indeed have to 'rough it'.

She had expressed a desire to go there at least a year before. Like many European intellectuals, she wanted to see democracy in action, 'to witness the actual working of republican institutions.'[12] Her visit would take the form of a sociological investigation – the first of its kind. And although she later made out that she decided to write up her findings in a book only weeks after her return to England, it is clear from statements like, 'this country shall know something more than it does [at present] of the *principles* of American institutions,' that it was in fact long premeditated (and well prepared).[13] What is more, she clearly wished to dissociate herself from works like Basil Hall's 1829 *Travels in North America* and Fanny Trollope's 1832 *Domestic Manners of the Americans*. Their books were highly subjective, and their snobbery roused much ill-feeling and even deep offence on the other side of the Atlantic. HM planned rather to impartially assess America by the degree to which it lived up to its declared republican intentions.* Given her indifference to the feelings of authorities, such a project did not bode well: to this day the Americans remain highly sensitive to any foreign criticism of their society and institutions.

There was also a major obstacle in the way of success. HM set out to observe 'THINGS' (as she put it), 'using THE DISCOURSE OF PERSONS as a commentary upon them.'[14] The *things* she observed were institutions of all kinds, from political ones in Washington down to local prisons and schools for deaf, blind and dumb

---

* Before his trip in 1842, Dickens read widely and found HM's *Society in America* and *Retrospect of Western Travel* to be the best books that had been written on America.

children (an area in which America had a lead over Britain at the time).* The *discourse of persons* she aimed to collect through talking with everyone, from the President down to a black slave girl sitting at her feet. She was particularly keen to hear what women talked about among themselves as they went about their daily lives. (We might note here that Alexis de Tocqueville, who researched and published his *Démocratie en Amérique* at just this time, spoke only with educated white men, and in uncertain English at that; ever since, Americans have preferred his book to HM's because it is less critical of their society.) But from the age of twelve or so, HM had been progressively losing her hearing; by 1834, at the age of thirty-two, she was so deaf that she could understand only what was spoken directly into the cup of her speaking tube. So her interlocutor had to be close beside her; general conversation in the vicinity was lost to her. (The speaking tube had one advantage: like whispering into someone's ear, it brought a sense of intimacy, which favoured greater frankness than conversation that could be overheard.) Her deafness also made it hard for her to carry out the simple interactions associated with travel, from reserving a seat on a stage coach to enquiring the way in the street.

HM was the first high-profile woman to make no effort to hide her disability, but rather to demand acceptance on an equal footing with everyone else. To reduce the strain that her deafness put on social intercourse, she had very early taken a life-long resolution *never to ask what had just been said.* So to conduct a sociological investigation in America, she needed someone at her side who could observe, listen, select, and summarize at any

---

* In *Retrospect of Western Travel,* HM pointed out that deaf and dumb children 'are far more numerous than is generally supposed. In 1830 the total number of deaf and dumb, of all ages, in the United States, was 6106. Of a teachable age the number was 2000; of whom 466 were in course of education. The number of deaf-mutes in Europe at the same time was 140,000' (Volume 3, p.94).

moment she chose whatever was of interest or relevance to her purposes, at the same time as acting as her research assistant and booking agent.

There was yet another obstacle in the way of her venture: HM had lost almost all sense of taste and smell; she needed a companion with the social skill to make innocent remarks like 'Oh, don't the flowers smell nice!' or 'Oh, that's very tasty!' to compensate for her own inability to comment. In short, she needed a super-companion, a sociable and intellectual alter ego who thought like her and knew exactly what she wanted, *without being prompted*. Failing this, HM's social interactions would have been greatly curtailed and her investigation severely handicapped. As it was, Americans who disliked her opinions maintained that her deafness disqualified her from writing about their country.

So she engaged a companion of much her own age, 'Miss J', as HM called her in her *Autobiography*; I shall continue to do so, as a mark of respect and also to distinguish her from all the other women in this account. First of all, Miss J had to learn what kind of information to pick out and memorize. At that time, no method of sociological enquiry had yet been formulated: Emile Durkheim's *Rules of Sociological Method* came out only in 1895, sixty years later. So during the crossing to America, which lasted all of forty-two days, HM drafted an essay on 'How to Observe', out of which grew her manual of methodology, *How to Observe Morals and Manners,* published 1838. Miss J must have rapidly understood and done just what was asked of her, for HM wrote in her *Autobiography,*

> Happily for me a lady of very superior qualifications, who was eager to travel, but not rich enough to indulge her desire, offered to go with me, as companion and helper, if I would bear her expenses. She paid her own voyages, and I the rest; and most capitally she fulfilled her share of the compact. Not only well educated but remarkably clever, and, above all, supremely

rational, and with a faultless temper, she was an extraordinary boon as a companion. She was as conscientious as able and amiable. She toiled incessantly to spare my time, strength and faculties. She managed the business of travel, and was for ever on the watch to supply my want of ears, – and, I may add, my defects of memory. Among the multitudes of strangers whom I saw, and the concourse of visitors who presented themselves every where, I should have made hourly mistakes but for her. She seemed to make none, – so observant, vigilant and reten- tive were her faculties. We fulfilled the term of our compact without a shadow of failure, but rather with large supereroga- tion* of good works on her part.[15]

Coming from HM, who always spoke her mind and eschewed flattery, this is praise of the highest order, unequalled through- out her published writings. She was not only the most intelligent woman of her time, she was endowed with an exceptional memory. That she should admit to 'defects of memory' is aston- ishing. So who was this paragon of travelling companions-cum- research assistants, and how did they meet?

Fortunately, HM let slip a 'Louisa' from time to time in *Retrospect of Western Travel*, in her *Autobiography,* and in her letters. (They have only recently been collected, for she made it a condition of corresponding with her that both parties should destroy the letters they received; and in her Will she forbade the publication of her correspondence.) So far as I know, the first to fully identify Miss J in print was Herbert McLachlan in his book about John Relly Beard (1800–76) and his descendants, *Records of a Family,* which was published by Manchester University Press in 1935. There, almost in passing, he wrote: 'the companion and friend of Harriet Martineau on her American travels' was 'Louisa Caroline, daughter of the Rev. John Jeffery of Billingshurst.'[16] I have not checked all the biographies of HM, but Vera Wheatley's

* That is, Miss J had done far more than was asked of her.

Life and Work of Harriet Martineau, which appeared in 1957, confirms this identification. In the twenty-first century, however, Miss J has been badly served by scholars who should certainly know better: in Linda H. Peterson's 2007 edition of HM's *Autobiography,* she states that Miss J was 'a daughter of Francis Jeffrey (1773–1850) whom [HM] had met in London.'[17] It takes only a moment's research to ascertain that Lord Jeffrey had only one daughter and her name was not Louisa.* Another American scholar, Deborah Anna Logan, who has been editing HM's letters, persistently spells Miss J's name both 'Jeffery' and 'Jeffrey'.† Miss J deserves better than this; so I decided to do what no one had ever attempted before and recover what I could of her life.[18]

McLachlan was correct: Miss J's father, John Jeffery (born in December 1779) was indeed the incumbent of the Baptist – soon to become Unitarian – chapel in Billingshurst, a village seven or eight miles (12km) from Horsham, in West Sussex. His parents,

* Feeling that Prof. Peterson cannot be trusted as an editor, I have used the first edition of HM's *Autobiography* for my quotations; it has the added advantage of being freely available on the internet.

† For instance, in Logan's edition of Maria Weston Chapman's *Memorials of Harriet Martineau,* she spells the name differently on pages 497 (note 32) and 499 (note 66); in both instances she is identifying Miss J, naming her husband and daughter. To judge by Deborah Logan's collections of HM's letters, HM regularly slipped up too – but since Logan herself is inconsistent, we cannot know whether the variation is in fact hers rather than HM's. It is, after all, standard editorial practice to adopt a uniform spelling of a person's name throughout a collection of letters, correcting the writer's mistakes. Logan does not do this, nor does she discuss her decision – if it was one – to admit variation. When we remember that HM had relatives called Jeffery and was acquainted with Lord Jeffrey, this results in frequent possibilities for misunderstanding, not to say confusion. Herbert McLachlan, who is generally a reliable source, spells the name 'Jeffrey', but Jeffery Watson, who is descended from Miss J's uncle, assures me that his family has always used 'Jeffery', and I shall use it here.

John Jeffery (I)* and Ann (née Caffyn or Caffin), married at Billingshurst in 1774. They had two sons, John (II) and Richard, and four surviving daughters, of whom Eliza (born in 1789) and Ruth (born in 1796) are of interest to us here. John (II) studied for two years at the General Baptist Academy in Islington, run by the Rev. John Evans, and then returned to Billingshurst. There, inspired no doubt by his father's activity as a maltster,[19] 'he soon afterwards embarked in the brewing business on an extensive scale,' although 'a considerable portion of his time was devoted to the work of the ministry,' which he carried out 'almost gratuitously.'[20] His brother Richard and a cousin, Isaac Jeffery, joined him in building the brewery, but they overestimated the demand; by 1812 they were obliged to put the business up for sale; the associated 'large dwelling-house, suitable for a family,' was sold by auction in January 1815. Creditors were still being paid off in 1829.[21]

In the meantime, the Rev. John Jeffery had married, on 18 October 1805, Louisa Caroline Taylor, born on 11 December 1783. She was the 'eldest daughter of William Taylor, Esq.,† of Tottenham Court Road, and granddaughter to the late Rev. Henry Taylor, well known for his celebrated defence of the Arian doctrine ... and many other valuable theological pieces.'[22] She had eight younger siblings: two brothers and six sisters.

Louisa Caroline's father, William Taylor (1755–1843), had been apprenticed in silk throwing – the process of turning raw silk into twisted thread for weaving – alongside George Courtauld (I) (1761–1823), but he chose rather to develop a tinsmith and ironmongery shop and warehouse in London in association with a Mr Jones. George Courtauld, on the other hand, remained in the production of silk, without (it must be said) much success.

---

* I am observing the convention of distinguishing between relatives having the same name by means of roman numerals.

† The Taylors of Norwich, from whom Harriet Martineau was descended, were quite unrelated to this family.

It was his eldest son Samuel (1793–1881), who made Courtaulds a household name. In the meantime, William Taylor married Courtauld's sister Catherine, the first of a long series of alliances between the two families that is cited as a prime example of nineteenth-century economic, social and religious networks formed by inter-marriage.* William Taylor's son Peter Alfred Taylor (I) married George Courtauld's daughter Catherine (known as Kate); and William's youngest daughter Ellen married Courtauld's son Samuel. As both the Taylors and the Courtaulds had many children, the combined families formed a large community in themselves, which increased through inter-marriage from generation to generation. Miss J's mother, on the other hand, was doing her own thing when she married a clergy-man quite unconnected with the Courtaulds or the Taylors (so far as I know), although he was rapidly welcomed into the extended family.

As the Taylor-Courtauld constellation is key to this story, we need to know more about it. The Courtauld silk business really started in 1816, when the young Samuel Courtauld (III) took over from his father and established a new mill at Braintree in Essex. He had done a business apprenticeship with Jones, Taylor & Co in London, and was soon joined by William Taylor's son, Peter Alfred Taylor (I), who had also trained in his father's firm; they formed Courtauld & Taylor in 1817. Although the early years were hard going, the second half of the nineteenth century saw the firm – as just 'Courtaulds' – become one of Britain's most successful textile companies, thanks especially to the fashion (fuelled by Queen Victoria in her long widowhood) for wearing black crape as a sign of mourning. By introducing innovative man-made fibres like viscose and rayon, Courtaulds survived and prospered right to the end of the twentieth century as one

---

* In *Thicker than Water: Siblings and Their Relations, 1780–1920*, Leonore Davidoff prints an eloquent chart illustrating this practice in the Taylor and Courtauld families.

of the largest textile companies in the world and the principal British manufacturer of women's underwear.

In view of the history of Courtaulds, and the most favourable comments that HM later made about Samuel Courtauld (III), it is instructive to read what George Courtauld (I) wrote about him in December 1816, when he was first setting up as a mill owner at the age of twenty-three: 'Humanly speaking, Samuel can scarcely fail of succeeding; [he has] so much intelligence and caution – such indefatigable application and high principles of rectitude – with evidently honourable, open and liberal dealing.' What is more, he devotes 'a very unusual personal attention to all the minutiae of his business.' In fact, he has 'so *many* advantages that I *cannot* doubt his overcoming *all* the difficulties he may meet with.'[23] The emphases are in the original. Few fathers who write flatteringly of a son setting out in life can have been proved so thoroughly right as George Courtauld.

We might observe here that the Courtauld family, originally Huguenots, were Unitarians, and politically radical; so too were the later Taylors: Peter Alfred Taylor (II) became an MP and, among other things, supported women's suffrage. In the eighteenth century, there had been the goldsmith Samuel Courtauld (I) and his wife Louisa Perina (I); she was a silversmith who ran the family business for many years after the early demise of her husband. They were the parents and grandparents of the Courtaulds who feature in this history. The Martineaus, too, were Unitarians of Huguenot origin. The love of freedom and the intelligence that they shared with the Courtaulds may well derive from this source. HM's father was also in the cloth industry, having a mill in Norwich. Unlike Courtauld & Taylor, however, Mr Martineau's business collapsed in the 1820s, leaving his family impoverished. As we shall see, Miss J was to suffer comparable misfortune.

Both the Courtauld and the Taylor families left us printed records of their lives and times. Miss J's cousin, Peter Alfred

Taylor (II), compiled and edited *Some Account of the Taylor Family*, which was 'printed for private circulation' in an edition of one hundred copies in 1875. Despite the scope of the book – which begins with the fourteenth century – and the editor's determination not to say anything personal about anyone living at the time of writing, it enables us to place Miss J among the Taylors. In the Courtauld family, randomly preserved letters were assembled by an anonymous editor and printed, again for private circulation, in 1916. The only complete set of all eight volumes of *Courtauld Family Letters* that is accessible to the public is in the British Library (and it has not been scanned). Most of my information about Miss J, prior to her visit to America, is extrapolated from the brief mentions of her in these two sources. That said, we can begin the story of her life.

Following his marriage in 1805, the Rev. John Jeffery brought his wife back to Billingshurst; their daughter, named Louisa Caroline after her mother, was born in Horsham, on 10 August 1806. (HM was four years older.) However, Mrs Jeffery died of consumption on 3 January 1808, aged just twenty-four. In a notice printed in *The Athenaeum* later that year, she was described as 'endowed with an excellent and cultivated understanding, a kind and affectionate disposition, and a mind in every respect calculated to promote and insure domestic felicity. She has left an infant daughter.'[24] At the time, it was most unusual for the death of a young woman to be noticed in this manner.

Her parents long grieved their loss. In 1810, William Taylor wrote to his wife Catherine of how, when riding close to where his family had lived when their daughter was alive, 'the whole scene brought to my Mind my dear Louisa so forcibly that my Yearning Heart was only relieved by floods of tears.'[25] It was doubtless some consolation, though, that his granddaughter, our Miss J, soon showed signs of taking after her mother. On 30 August 1811, when Miss J had just turned five, Sophia Courtauld (I), Miss J's great aunt, observed to Catherine Taylor: 'by your account and by all accounts, dear John Jeffery's little girl seems like her own dear mother become a child again.'[26] She was no doubt very precious to both families.

I have found no record of Miss J's early life. Given the remarks just quoted, she surely spent some time with her Taylor grand-parents. When their eldest daughter died, all their other children were still under twenty-one; the youngest, Ellen, was not yet eight. Miss J may also have spent some time with her father's family; his sisters Jane, Eliza, Rebecca, and Ruth Jeffery were respectively twenty, eighteen, sixteen, and eleven years old when Mrs Jeffery died. Miss J certainly had abiding affection for her youngest aunt, Ruth, as we shall see.

Regular contact with the Courtaulds seems to have begun when Miss J was eight. After the failure of his brewery, John Jeffery sought more pupils for the school alongside his chapel, doing most of the teaching himself; George Courtauld (I) sent him his two younger sons, George Courtauld (II), born 1802, and John Courtauld, born 1807. They arrived in Billingshurst in February 1814. At this point his eldest son Samuel (III) – soon to become Miss J's uncle by marrying her aunt Ellen – encouraged little George by telling him of his full confidence in John Jeffery.[27]

A few months later, their big sister Kate exclaimed to George in a letter, 'What a sweet girl your cousin Louisa is! I never knew so fine-tempered a child – she must be a great acquisition to you all.' (Kate sounds very grown up for a girl just a month short of her nineteenth birthday, and she was aware of it: 'I am afraid you will think me grown quite a *fine lady* when you know I have two or three times almost *fainted*' – the underlining is hers). She adds, significantly, 'Cousin Peter is just come from Braintree' (the Courtauld home): she married her cousin Peter Alfred Taylor (I) – one of Miss J's two Taylor uncles – four years later.[28]

So, still taking after the mother she had lost so young, Miss J was noticeably good-natured by the age of eight. We can also infer from Kate's use of the word *acquisition* that her cousin had just rejoined the Billingshurst household after living elsewhere for a time. And she would only make this comment after meeting Miss J for the first time. Her letter is headed 'Frederick Place 36', the home of Miss J's grandparents, in Hampstead Road, London;* Kate must have met her there.

Little George was less impressed by his cousin, so Kate remonstrated with him the following year, by which time he was at Mill Hill academy (which he compared unfavourably with his time in Billingshurst): 'I am surprised you did not particularly like your little cousin Louisa Jeffery; she is a charming girl – she is here now and sends her love to you.'[29] On this occasion Kate was writing from 'Streatham Cottage', of which more in a moment.

The Jefferys were known to the local gentry, principally the Eversheds around Billingshurst,† and the Dendys near Horsham. The Eversheds were staunch supporters of the Baptist chapel in Billingshurst, which had been founded by an Evershed in 1754. In May 1815 George Courtauld (I) asked his son George to 'remember me to Miss [Eliza] Jeffery and to those who enquire after me – particularly to the family of the Eversheds – where you know I passed a day when I was last at Billingshurst.'[30] He was doubtless introduced to the Eversheds by John Jeffery.

But Miss J's father was a sick man. Around 1810 he developed 'an affection of the chest, which rendered his articulation scarcely audible' and progressively prevented him from preaching.

Yet his zeal for the improvement of his congregation was not

---

* William and Catherine Taylor moved to Frederick Place in 1813, leaving the ironmongery business to his ex-partner, Mr Jones.

† In 1851, the Rev. John Jeffery's niece Sophia, the daughter of his young sister Rebecca and David Brent Price, married a John Evershed. Both of Miss J's children kept in contact with this family and left legacies to them.

diminished; he still watched over them with a truly pastoral affection.... When his voice became so low that he could not be heard by those who were only a short distance from him, he was accustomed to express his thoughts in writing for the benefit of his flock. His papers ... were read to them either by one of his amiable sisters, or some other friend.[31]

By the spring of 1815, his condition was cause for alarm.

Good wishes for his health flowed in from the Courtaulds, and eight-year-old John was enjoined not to 'do anything to vex or make [his teacher] uneasy: that would be a sad thing indeed when he is sick; it would be bad enough when he is well.'[32] (The previous winter, John had been kept at school during the Christmas holidays, for he was not an assiduous pupil, and on one occasion he had been punished for 'no less than setting the whole school laughing while Mr Jeffery was instructing them!!!'[33]) As spring turned to summer, he declined rapidly; George Courtauld (I) collected his sons from Billingshurst on 30 May 1815, recording that John Jeffery remained 'peculiarly resigned and cheerful.' He expired a fortnight later, 'retaining the full use of all his faculties until within a few minutes of his death.'[34]

This left Miss J a penniless, homeless orphan at the age of nine, but an orphan with two large families concerned for her welfare. Two months earlier, Ruth Courtauld had told her son George at Billingshurst to pass on her

> most affectionate regards to your kind, good master [i.e. John Jeffery], and tell him how happy I should be to welcome his Louisa too to our habitation and try in some small degree to return some of his kindness to my dear boys. I wish we could prevail on him to bring you all to us. I am going to have a Dicky and Dicky cart [i.e. a donkey and donkey cart] and we shall have such fine rides.

Later, she added, 'I have made a nice Summer house where I hope we shall all drink tea.'[35]

The invitation was accepted and after John Jeffery's death his sisters Ruth and Eliza, along with little Miss J, went to stay with the Courtaulds.[36] Ruth did not remain long. She was not quite twenty; her family had lost money in the brewery and she needed to fend for herself. This was probably the moment when she set up a school of her own, or joined some other woman with a school that she later took over. At any rate, we know from McLachlan that at Ruth Jeffery's school, which was situated in or close to Horsham, Miss J formed a lifelong friendship with a fellow pupil, Mary Barnes, who had been born in Portsmouth on 3 November 1802.[37] (More of her in due course.)

Eliza stayed on, participating in the Courtaulds' family life by baking a cake to send to little George at his boarding school. Early that autumn, however, she too fell 'very dangerously ill'. Her recovery began only in December. In mid-January 1816, George Courtauld (I) reported from their home in Braintree to his daughter Sophia (the main recipient of the Courtauld letters) that 'Miss Jeffery continues mending:– tho' very slowly; we removed her in a litter yesterday from her room at the Cottage to our house for the advantage of fire and air.' And his wife added, 'Miss J [i.e. Eliza] is now much better and likes Sam's room much better than the Cottage.'[38] (I think this is the Streatham Cottage mentioned earlier; it seems to have served as an annexe to the Courtauld home.) On 29 January 1816, Sophia wrote to George at school: 'Eliza Jeffery desires her love to you, and she is just come downstairs for the first time, and continues to improve.'[39] In February 1816, she was 'still mending, though slowly.'[40] Only in March could Kate report that 'E[liza] J[effery] is just gone to Billingshurst, very far from well yet.'[41] She did not recover: she died on 20 May the following year.

In all this time, the only mention in the *Courtauld Family Letters* of the newly orphaned Miss J came on 23 March 1816 when Kate sent her love to George: she had quite possibly been with the Courtaulds ever since her father's death, doing her best to help care for her aunt Eliza. She was present at Sophia's eigh-teenth birthday party on 11 August 1817, along with other members of the family.[42] (I hope they were celebrating her birth-day too: she turned eleven the day before.) In November that year, Samuel Courtauld (III) mentions her (as 'L.J.') in the same breath as his sister Kate and his young brothers, George and John, who were 'all well,' which suggests that she was in all like-lihood still living with them at that time. The following month, her grandmother Catherine, Mrs William Taylor, was looking forward welcoming home her daughters Anna and Ellen (who were by now twenty-four and sixteen respectively) along with Miss J; Kate and Peter Alfred Taylor (I) were to join them later, probably for Christmas. At this point, however, Miss J disap-pears from the *Courtauld Family Letters* for several years; my guess is that she went to live with her aunt Ruth, to pursue her education at her school.

There was a good reason why she did not remain with the Courtaulds: they were preparing to go to America. George Courtauld (I) had first gone out there in 1785, planning to set up a silk mill, but he soon turned to acquiring land suitable for farming. Having met a congenial Irishman, Stephen Minton, he paid a brief visit to the Minton family in Kanturk, County Cork, and then both men, along with Stephen's sister Ruth Minton, returned to the backwoods of America. George and Ruth married 'at the house of Cornelius Cayler on the Mohawk River, State of New York' on 10 July 1789.[43] Four or five years later, they returned to England with their first two children, Louisa Perina (II) and Samuel (III), plus 'a couple of hundred pounds, clear of all incumbrances;' they left two estates, each of 300 acres, to be developed as farmland.[44] Their six other children were born in England and Ireland.

Back home, George tried to develop the silk business in Essex, but he remained a restless pioneer at heart and by 1818 he was off again. He bought almost 6000 acres of uncultivated land about twenty miles from what was then called Englishtown, Ohio – it is now subsumed within East Nelsonville, in the Appalachians – and returned home (paddling all the way down to the coast, solo, in a canoe) to take his unwilling family out there. It was August 1820 when he set off for the New World once more, along with his children Eliza, Sophia, George (II) and John, leaving Samuel at the silk mill. His wife Ruth, who knew all too well the hardships of the settler's life, steadfastly refused to return to America. His eldest daughter Louisa Perina (II) embarked in London with the others, only to jump ship at Gravesend with just her hand luggage, leaving the rest of it in the ship's hold. His daughter Kate also stayed home: she had married Peter Alfred Taylor (I) in September 1818, and their son Peter was born in July 1819. Less than two years later, however, they left little Peter with his grandmother Ruth, and joined the emigrants on the banks of the Hockhocking River. Then they established a brewery in Gallipolis, about fifty miles from Englishtown.

Conditions in 'the backwoods' were primitive; in 1819, George Courtauld (I) described Englishtown itself as comprising 'about eighty houses, of which about a dozen are brick, the rest frame, or log.'[45] In the tavern – the most civilized building after the courthouse – as much light came in through gaps in the unplastered walls and ceiling as through the windows. There was no sanitation or water supply. Infections and disease debilitated all the Courtauld family. The unbroken land on their estate proved impossible to plough without borrowing extra horses from a neighbour, who could not, or would not, spare them. The family split up and sought work in neighbouring settlements. George (I) died of a malarial type of infection on 13 August 1823; his children regrouped and dragged themselves home, wracked with fever and ague. Ironically, their father had seen this American venture as a way 'to prepare for you all a comfortable Azylum, in case of public or private disasters' at home.[46] (The years following the defeat of Napoleon at Waterloo were socially unsettled in England, with fears of revolution in the air; in 1819 a peaceful demonstration in Manchester calling for political reform was dispersed with much bloodshed by cavalrymen wielding sabres, an event ironically named Peterloo.)

Meanwhile, George's wife Ruth had been seeking suitable people to accompany her grandson Peter across the Atlantic to rejoin his parents. Hearing that two of the Evershed family's sons, John and Thomas, were thinking of emigrating, she asked Miss J (not quite seventeen by this time) to enquire about it. She reported back in June 1823 that they had 'entirely given up all thought of settling in America.'[47] This was fortunate for little Peter (who turned five in July that year): given the slow speed of communications at that time, it would have been very hard to arrange for him to meet up with his parents, of whom he had no memory, as they made their weary way back from Gallipolis: their paths might even have crossed in mid-Atlantic!

Miss J's youngest aunt Ellen had married Samuel Courtauld (III) in July 1822, making them her closest Taylor-Courtauld relatives, and it is clear that she was in regular contact with them, if not actually living with them. (Given that Ellen was less than five years older than Miss J, she was probably more like a big sister than an aunt to her.) During the American interlude, Samuel had built up the silk business and his brothers joined him in it when they came back. George (II) turned out to have a gift for inventing improvements to their machines, and together with their brother-in-law Peter Alfred Taylor (I), they brought the firm through the slump of the late 1820s.

As for Samuel's sisters, occupations had to be found for them too. At this time, unmarried young women were a financial burden to their families, so if they were not employed else-where, they had to be *useful* to their family. They could expect to be called upon, like Anne Eliot in Jane Austen's *Persuasion*, to step in at a moment's notice when an elderly relative needed a companion or a nurse, when a mother fell sick, or a child fell out of an apple tree. While her family was in America, Louisa Perina Courtauld (II) worked in Scotland as a governess for £10 a year. By comparison, Courtauld & Taylor's mill hands – all of them young women but for a few men working as overseers, carpenters, etc. – who had finished their apprenticeships were paid six, seven or even eight shillings a week in 1816, an average of £17.50 a year.[48] Unlike a governess, however, they had to pay for their own food and lodging out of this. Miss J, on the other hand, who was rapidly approaching the age at which she would have to prove herself useful, was no longer penniless: her great uncle Henry Taylor, who died without issue in 1822, left her a life interest in a trust fund of £1000. That will have brought her something like £40 a year – not a fortune by any means, but at least she no longer had to count on her relatives to clothe her or put pennies in her purse.

In January 1824, shortly after the Courtaulds came home, Miss J's aunt Christiana Fox Taylor, who had married Daniel Lambert (1776–1857), the scion of a family of utmost respectability,* seated in Surrey since the time of Edward II, invited Sophia Courtauld, who had taught in a small school when she was in America, to come and 'instruct' her children. Between 1813 and 1826, Aunt Christiana bore eight sons and one daughter, so there was plenty of work for a governess. She offered 'sixty guineas per annum, washing included.'[49] Sophia could hardly refuse such munificence; she lived with the Lamberts for almost two years.

During those two years, Miss J seems to have spent much time with her grandparents, William and Catherine Taylor; at any rate she was with them on holiday in Harwich in 1825 when they were joined by her little cousin Peter Alfred Taylor (II).[50]

---

* Daniel Lambert's grandfather, the politician Sir Daniel Lambert (1685–1780), was knighted by George II for his services to the State, but died of 'gaol fever', i.e. typhus, caught from prisoners while sitting on the Bench at the Old Bailey.

She remained with them during her grandmother's last months – Catherine died on 17 June 1826 – and was still at their house in London in October 1826.[51]

Early in 1827, she took over Sophia's job as governess to the Lambert children. In March, her aunt Christiana reported to Sophia,

> You will be gratified to hear that we go on extremely well in the school, and I may say out of the school too. Louisa is all I could possibly wish her to be; she seems extremely pleased and satisfied with Chrissie [almost fifteen], and C is equally pleased and contented and seems to be attached to Louisa. Willy [aged seven] is very little in the nursery, and is very good; Anna [aged five-and-a-half] is more occupied in the school and has begun Geography. She was told she lived in Great Britain and the next day, on being desired to say where she lived, she stopped for a moment and then said, 'I live in large Britain.'[52]

Aunt Christiana will have been all the more grateful to Miss J when she suffered from chronic headaches. In fact, all the Lamberts seem to have been prone to sickness.

To start with, there were the usual childhood illnesses, of course: in July 1827, when the eldest son Daniel was thirteen-and-a-half, the fourth son Henry was eight-and-a-half and the next son Alfred was just four, they all had scarlet fever. 'Louisa is a most kind and attentive nurse to them and consequently takes much fatigue from me,' reported Christiana.[53] In the late 1830s Miss J also tended the next-to-youngest son Nicholas who died in 1840, aged sixteen. In later years, Daniel, who became a lawyer, was 'a thorough gentleman, a most amiable and upright man,' but 'the want of a very strong physical health prevented him from being as widely known as his abilities and attainments deserved.'[54] He died at the age of forty-five.

What is striking in these Courtauld letters is that almost every time Miss J is mentioned, there is a positive comment about her, and never a word of complaint. No one else is so privileged. As

Kate (Mrs P. A.) Taylor put it in 1837, when Christiana had 'another of her attacks' of acute headache, 'L. J. is with her – oh she would be a treasure to many a one.'[55] In the volume about the Taylor family, there is mention of a similar treasure: Betty Butterly, born around 1750. She married Miss J's great uncle Peter Taylor, a clergyman with a degree from Cambridge. On 24 June 1782, Miss J's grandfather William Taylor described his sister-in-law in these terms:

> I look upon her to be one of the most worthy, most rational women in the world; the more you are acquainted with her, the more will you esteem her. She has indeed many good qualities which are not possessed by either of my Sisters, who are nevertheless both amiable women.[56]

Quite clearly, Miss J had similar qualities. (Remember that HM called her 'supremely rational'.) Betty – called 'Aunt P' by the Taylor family – had no children and outlived her husband by almost forty years. Peter Alfred Taylor (II) recalled her as 'a kindly, gracious old lady. Her face was one of those which, in old age, *puckers* up into thousand wrinkles, and there seemed a smile in each!'[57] I do not know how often Miss J visited her, but she was certainly at Aunt P's bedside when she died in 1837, for it was she who notified her relatives in London of the event.[58]

From the fragmentary evidence provided by the *Courtauld Family Letters,* I have the impression that Miss J began to feel restless in the early 1830s. In December 1830, Maria Minton* complained that she had 'not lately heard of dear Louisa – I heard she no longer received any income from Sam and was looking for a situation.'[59] (I know nothing about the 'income

---

* Maria was the daughter of a John Minton, by his first wife Henrietta Leycester, so she was related to George Courtauld's wife Ruth (née Minton). Maria was born in New York in August 1796, which makes her just ten years older than Miss J. According to Burke's *Genealogical and Heraldic History of the Landed Gentry,* Vol. 2 (1847), she married Robert George Maunsell (as his second wife) on 29 October 1834.

from Sam.' It is possible, though, that Maria was referring not to
Miss J but to Louisa Perina Courtauld (II).) A year later, she was
absent from the Lamberts' for a full month at least; the next
mention of her comes only in April 1833, when Kate told Sophia
that she had 'seen Loo and Ruth Jeffery today.'[60] Shortly after
that, Miss J was visiting Kate in company with a Mrs Evershed.[61]
I would guess this to be Louisa Evershed, who was a friend of
Sophia Courtauld (II). So Miss J had renewed contact with
people from the Billingshurst and Horsham area where she was
born. Then on 8 July 1833, there's an enigmatic exclamation from
Maria Minton: 'Poor Louisa: I do not like to think of her – oh
how different from what we once hoped with good apparent
reason.'[62] Had Miss J been spurned by a man who once seemed
interested in her, or (which seems more likely) had she received
a proposal and turned her suitor down? That would be con-
sonant with her need to consult with her closest relatives and
family friends (for lack of any living parent).

The next letter – also dated July 1833 – from Maria to Sophia
reads: 'I shall be anxious to hear what Louisa does – to have her
go far away would I think be a trial to Aunt, altho' being near
may bring continued uneasiness.'[63] If the rejected suitor was
someone close to the Lambert family, that would explain the
'continued uneasiness.' It looks as though Miss J was seeking an
elegant way out of an uncomfortable situation. The opportunity
to travel for two years with HM, who was at this very moment
voicing her intention of visiting America – the letter in which
she mentions writing a book about American institutions is
dated 29 August 1833 – must have come at just the right time.

In a letter dated 12 December 1833, HM wrote, 'There is no
lack of people who wish to go with me.'[64] Two months later, she
told an American whom she planned to visit, 'I shall probably
be joined by a lady who wishes to travel in your country with
objects somewhat resembling mine.'[65] Was this 'lady' Miss J? In
her edition of HM's *Collected Letters,* Deborah Logan assumes

that it was, without offering any supporting evidence. As for Miss J's aims or 'objects' in visiting America, in addition to 'getting away from it all', she was surely keen to see the country that everyone talked about and that the Courtaulds had tried and rejected.

Now we can address the question of how HM and Miss J came into contact with each other.

&

HM was brought up in Norwich, about twice as far to the north-east of London as Billingshurst is to the south-west of it. Braintree, where the Courtauld family lived beside their mills, lies roughly one third of the way between London and Norwich. Had she and Miss J met on a stage coach, I am sure it would have been remembered and recorded. (As it was, English people of their class did not generally make acquaintances in the stage coach; they studiously ignored each other, for lack of an introduction.) Their social and intellectual circles, on the other hand, overlapped.

In 1822, HM's brother James, three years her junior, began his training as a Unitarian minister at Manchester College, which was then situated in York. He introduced HM to several of the two dozen or so scholars attending the College at that time, and she became engaged to one of them, but he died before their marriage could be celebrated. This, in itself, tells us how many unrecorded interactions must have taken place between HM and the students at York. Like all young scholars, they ranged from the light-hearted and playful (given to pranks), to the more sober, serious and studious; the former were dubbed 'sinners'; the latter 'saints'. James, who had been 'an unusually grave and thoughtful little boy,' 'was counted chief of the '"saints".' His best friend (and rival for the annual prizes) was John Relly Beard (1800–76), who 'was regarded as the idol of the "sinners".'[66] Another of the students was William Gaskell (1805–84); he was

Beard's best friend, close collaborator and life-long colleague. After Manchester College moved to London in 1853, they co-founded a similar training school for Unitarian ministers in Manchester. (It is still there.) Gaskell married Elizabeth Stevenson, who is now universally known as the novelist Mrs Gaskell – with whom HM exchanged many letters.

But let us not lose sight of John Relly Beard. He became a much-respected minister, educator, theologian, translator and prolific writer, not as well known as James Martineau, of course, who for forty-five years was 'Professor of Mental and Moral Philosophy and Political Economy' at the Unitarian College in the south of England. (He had to get 'Political Economy' into his title, for he was jealous of his sister.) Although their respective philosophies diverged increasingly as the years passed, the two remained life-long friends; Beard's eldest son Charles became a disciple and colleague of James's. And this is where we find a link with Miss J: in June 1826, Beard married the sweetheart of his teens, Mary Barnes – Miss J's best friend from her schooldays. It was a very successful marriage. 'Of all the blessings of my life,' observed Beard in his last letter to James, shortly before he died, 'my wife is the greatest.'[67]

Miss J kept up her friendship with Mary, visiting the Beards' home in Manchester – with consequences which I shall detail in due course. The friendship was reciprocal: Miss J's name lived on for a while in the tragically brief lives of the Beards' youngest daughters, Sophia Louisa (1841–45) and Annie Louisa Caroline (1846–56), and also in one of their grandchildren. It is uncanny that, of all the Beards' children, the one who bore both Miss J's names (coupled with that of her Beard grandmother) should have been the one who seems to have most closely resembled her in personality, being a sweet, 'engaging, loving child.' On Annie's death at the age of ten, even the poet and novelist George MacDonald (1824–1905), of *Phantastes* fame, wrote a letter of condolence to the Beards. 'I honoured and wondered at your child.... "Of such is the kingdom of Heaven".' John Relly Beard mourned Annie much as William Taylor had mourned the loss of Miss J's mother: 'Alas! The light of the house has been removed,' he wrote.[68]

HM would have been only half aware of Beard's wedding, for it took place down in Portsmouth while her father was on his deathbed, but Beard himself became an important figure for her. HM's first articles and stories were published, from 1822 onwards, in the Unitarian *Monthly Repository,* to which Beard was also a regular contributor. The first mention of Beard in her published letters comes only in April 1830, when she exclaimed to James over Beard's 'sincerity, zeal, sense, industry, and purity,'[69] and her articles show that she shared his ideas.

In a series of essays in the *Monthly Repository* on the state of modern Unitarianism, John Relly Beard issued a particular call for writers to make the faith more experiential and relevant to contemporary life. 'Unitarians have not moved forward with the general mass,' he wrote. 'They have ... not kept pace with the spirit of the age.' To this he added an appeal to all Unitarians: 'You are each a minister of Christ.' HM did what Beard preached. Her 1820s devotional books and tales show the 'practical divinity' of Unitarianism in young people's lives, and her *Monthly Repository* discursive essays always blend theory with practice. Martineau instructs readers how to live out specifically Unitarian theological principles in their daily lives and in their wider social involvement.[70]

For all this affinity of opinion, we unfortunately have no record of HM and Beard meeting in person; we know that they exchanged letters, although only two or three appear to have survived; one of them is still uncollected.

In 1835, Beard launched a monthly periodical of his own, *The Christian Teacher and Chronicle.* After two years, it was losing money that he could ill afford, so he printed an appeal for an increase in sales. HM wrote back:

Your note gave me great concern.... I promise you my best
support, if I live and am well. I will try to send you some kind of
article for every number, but cannot quite promise this.... In
five weeks I shall have done my book [presumably *Retrospect of
Western Travel*], and then I shall work for you again.[71]

The tone tells us that by now HM and Beard were on friendly
terms, and had been so for a while.

Also at this time, Beard included four of HM's hymns in his
Collection of Hymns for Public and Private Worship (1837). I would
suggest that HM's *The Hour and the Man* (1840), on Toussaint
Louverture, inspired Beard's *Life of Toussaint Louverture* (1853),
for in it he affirmed, 'Yes, here is the man, and the hour is
coming,' thus acknowledging her pioneering work.

But none of this provides us with the least hint that Mary
Beard might have introduced Miss J to HM (if only by letter). So
did they meet in London? It must be said at once that although
HM was determined to avoid being lionized by London society,
she could not help but meet people; since she was famous,
everyone who was anyone wished to be introduced to her and
claim her acquaintance.

The success of *Illustrations* had brought her so many letters
and parcels that the Norwich post office was overwhelmed and
asked her to send someone with a barrow to collect her daily
postbag. So in November 1832 she moved to London where she
could receive documents without recourse to the post. She could
also more easily research her stories, each one of which she
placed in a different, carefully crafted setting.

Prior to that date, HM had made only brief visits to town,
particularly to see William Johnson Fox (1786–1864), the editor
of the *Monthly Repository* who had encouraged her early writing,
and then to see his brother Charles after he became the publisher of the *Illustrations*. William Fox was an up-and-coming figure
in London, the Unitarian minister of South Place Chapel in
Finsbury, which had been built specifically for him. He made the

Chapel a meeting-place for progressive thinkers, writers, and feminists. The Taylors and Courtaulds, including Peter Alfred Taylor (I) and, later, his son Peter Alfred (II), all attended services there whenever they were in town. Unfortunately I have found no mention of South Place, or of Fox (at this time), in the Courtauld letters, so I can offer no precise dates here.

On the other hand, Fox had a daughter, Eliza (1824–1903), who much admired HM. In 1833, however, she was too young to be introducing Miss J, but in her late teens she became a friend of the Courtaulds (who called her Lieschen), particularly Sophia. We'll glimpse her again when we come to the 1840s.

In 1829, William Fox became the guardian of the two daughters of his good friend Benjamin Flower (1755–1829), the English radical journalist and political writer. (Flower's brother Richard was another who emigrated to America, where his son George founded Albion and the English Settlement in Illinois.) Although Flower's daughters Eliza (1803–46) and Sarah (1805–48) were of age when their father died, Fox was appointed their guardian. He welcomed them to his home, where they met HM. Eliza particularly liked her; a composer, she set the hymn written by HM that was sung at the memorial service for the Hindu reformist Ram Mohan Roy in South Place Chapel in October 1833.* Sarah Flower was a poet (best remembered for her hymn, 'Nearer My God to Thee'), painter and singer. On 15 November 1832 – the month when HM moved to London – Samuel Courtauld (III) told Sophia that he wished she 'knew the Flowers and Miss Martineau…. I saw them last Sunday' – would this have been at the Chapel? – 'and liked them prodigiously.'[72] (Sophia did get to know HM, as we shall see. Samuel came to

---

* In her own mind, HM associated Ram Mohan Roy with the first public recognition of her talent, for it was during the ceremony in South Place Chapel, on 25 May 1831, at which he was welcomed by the British and Foreign Unitarian Association, that she learned she had won its essay competition.

admire Fox; in 1847 he arranged for him to receive an annuity of
£400, which he enjoyed until his death in 1864.)

In my view, after Mary Beard, Kate (Mrs P. A.) Taylor is the
person most likely to have brought Miss J's name to the attention of HM, if not directly, then through one of the Flower
sisters: in March 1835 she noted, 'Miss Flower comes today.'[73]
Kate's off-hand manner suggests that this was by no means their
first contact. In June 1846 she mentioned that there had been a
time when she 'used to see' HM.[74] If Kate meant literally *seeing*
rather than *socially interacting with* HM, then she may have told
one of the Flower sisters about Miss J. (When, in August 1848,
HM wrote positively of making the acquaintance of Mr and Mrs
P. A. Taylor,[75] she must have been referring to Kate's son and his
wife Mentia.)

It is clear that, like almost everyone of any education, the
Taylor-Courtauld families had been aware of HM from the
moment the *Illustrations* began to appear: a friend of Sophia's,
Isabella Bell, told her: 'I hope your brothers have read Miss
Martineau's *Illustrations of Political Economy* – she is greatly
admired for the way in which she has simplified the subject.' As
Sophia had poor eyesight, Isabella went on, 'You must not look
into Miss Martineau: the type would not suit your eyes.'[76]
However, no further letter in the Courtauld collection mentions
HM before she left for America.

Whoever it was that told HM of Miss J, it must have been in
mid-1833, and I suspect that they came to agreement by letter.
They were certainly not well acquainted when they set out
together. Why otherwise would HM have felt the need to spell
out the 'great difficulties in joining a party for so very long a journey, extending over so long a time'? As though to justify her
choice of companion, she argued, 'To be with new friends is a
fearful risk under such an ordeal: and the ordeal is too severe, in

my opinion, to render it safe to subject an old friendship to it.'[77] Oscar Wilde put a similar thought into the mouth of Lady Bracknell: 'I am not in favour of long engagements. They give people the opportunity of finding out each other's character before marriage, which I think is never advisable.'[78] Better then to take a new companion, rather than an old friend – to start with a clean slate, so to speak. So it is quite possible that HM and Miss J first met in person only on the quayside at Liverpool, a day or two before they sailed on 9 August 1834.

Playing safe, HM had wished 'to leave the choice [of travelling companion or companions] open to near the last;' for her, nothing was finalized until shortly before they sailed.[79] On 30 May 1834, with just ten weeks to go, she invited two women (with whom she had already travelled) to accompany her, explaining that other friends of hers, having promised to come, were prevented by family circumstances.[80] But they declined the invitation. So rather than forming a party, it was to be just HM and Miss J, which I am sure was more efficient for information gathering, not to mention affording greater flexibility of movement.

Only one letter that Miss J wrote prior to leaving for America has survived. Penned from the Lamberts' home in Banstead on 2 July 1834, it is addressed to Sophia. Miss J apologizes for not having told her herself of her 'pleasant future prospects' – news of which must have spread like wildfire through the Taylor and Courtauld families – 'but the only letters I have written are answers to letters of business connected with my future arrangements.' I guess her chief correspondent was HM.

She intends to visit 'Grandpapa' William Taylor on 18 July, and hopes to see Sophia at Folley House – see the photograph on the following page – the next day. She goes on:

> I shall be grateful for any letters of introduction, provided I may use them or not, as I find convenient. I, of course, shall not arrange our route and therefore it may not be in my power to visit the residences of your friends.

An early photograph of Folley House*

The Courtaulds would of course be expecting her to visit their friends and relatives in America.

George Courtauld (I) had a younger brother, Samuel (II), who emigrated to Pennsylvania in the late-eighteenth century. He married into the Wharton family, direct descendants of the Thomas Wharton who had landed in Philadelphia in 1683. He had three daughters: Louisa (born in 1800), Amelia (1803), and Sarah (1806). Miss J may well have wished to meet them, for

---

* The spelling varies: Folley, Folly, and sometimes Foley House, in the hamlet of High Garrett, three miles (4.4km) north of Braintree, Essex. It had been bought by Samuel Courtauld (III) in 1824. Conveniently situated midway between his Braintree and Halstead mills, it was his family home for thirty-four years. The house is still there, having been, at various times in the last century-and-a-half, a Barnardo's home, and a residential care home for the deaf.

they were much her age, but that was not to be. Nor did she meet up with Louisa Perina Courtauld (II), who had emigrated alone to America three years before. Her time was not her own.

Her first duty was to accompany HM, whose appointments diary was well filled right from the start. As in London, everyone wished to meet her. HM exclaimed, 'all Philadelphia has called upon me – people of many ranks and all opinions, religious and political.' She and Miss J also visited various institutions there, including prisons, and interviewed the inmates. Miss J explained how things would be in her letter to Sophia (which would of course be passed all round the Courtauld family):

> Miss M has letters of introduction from the Chancellor to all the first people, [such] as [President] Jackson,* [Henry] Clay, [ex-Vice-President John] Calhoun, [ex-President James] Madison† and [Daniel] Webster....
>
> I will not promise to write to you when absent because I dislike to break a promise and I know how difficult it is for me to write when I am not quietly seated at home, but I know I ought to write to all my friends, as it is the only method I have of showing the gratitude I feel for all the kind interest they take in my welfare.[81]

She did write home, but only one letter from Miss J in America is described in the Courtauld collection; others are merely mentioned. On 26 February 1835, Kate (Mrs P. A.) Taylor reported to Sophia,

> I have just rec'd a long letter from Loo Jeffery which, when I

---

* Shortly after HM had interviewed him, Jackson survived an assassination attempt, the first against a President in office, as he was leaving a funeral in the Capitol which HM had attended, so she witnessed the arrest of the would-be assassin. Thus she learned that, although no prominent person in England is immune to attack, 'in America, the evil is sadly common' (*Autobiography,* Vol. 1, p.74).

† HM spent the best part of three days talking with 'the father of the Constitution'.

have answered, I will send you. She has seen Mr [Thomas] Ewing – who she says is very portly in person – she says he seems to be considered highly among the 2nd class of senators – I don't quite know what she means by this – [Daniel] Webster seems her grandee – but I have only yet read it once and there is so much of it I must read it again to have a distinct idea of her impressions. One thing is clear: she is delighted – indeed how could she be otherwise.... The Americans and Miss Martineau have evidently made up their minds to be mutually pleased and Miss M's book – which I presume will be the result of the visit – will be a very pleasing picture of them and therefore to them – whether altogether a fair one is a different question.[82]

Quite clearly, Kate was unaware of HM's determination to be perfectly objective and to speak her mind, whether it pleased the Americans or not.

Of more interest – for it provides us with a unique description of Miss J – is a letter to Sophia and Kate dated 30 July 1835 from their eldest sister, Louisa Perina (II):

I was in company with a clergyman the other day who said he had been travelling with two English ladies, a Miss Martin and a Miss – Smith perhaps; did I know them? No. One of them is an authoress and it is supposed they are travelling for the purpose of further publications. I said it was rather singular that two couple of English ladies should be travelling at the same time for a similar purpose in the U.S. as I was somewhat acquainted with a Miss Martineau and Jeffery lately come over, probably with some such views. No, that was not their names. Describe them, said I and so he gave an exact description of the elder and deaf lady and the dark, short, lively, loquacious younger.[83]

'Dark, short, lively and loquacious' – Miss J in four words.

Of even greater interest is a previously unnoticed (and therefore uncollected) letter dated 19 October 1834 – just one month after their arrival in New York – from HM to the Rev. and Mrs

Charles Brooks (who had been fellow passengers on the crossing from Liverpool). 'First, let me discharge a duty,' she writes,

> as well as give myself and you pleasure, by reporting of my companion, Louisa Jeffery. I am really delighted with her, and my esteem and regard for her grow every day. Our popularity so far I consider to be much owing to the cheerfulness and pleasantness of her manner. No difficulty or fatigue seems to have any effect upon her. She is as careful of me as my mother herself could be, and as a companion she is all I could wish, so great is her good sense joined with much cultivation of mind. I believe that she is much liked wherever we have been and am sure she ought to be.[84]

This 'duty' of reporting on Miss J suggests that, during the crossing, HM said something like, 'I'll tell you later what I think of her,' to Mrs Brooks. This supports my theory that, prior to their departure, HM and Miss J knew each other only by letter. We can also surmise that, given Miss J's cheerful and engaging manner, HM will have had no hesitation about taking her everywhere: her social ease must have smoothed things for HM. As we have seen, her high esteem for Miss J remained unchanged twenty years later when she wrote her *Autobiography*.

It is also striking that much of the letter is expressed in the first person plural – 'We saw all the beautiful scenery,' for instance – when HM was notorious for her use of the first person singular, which some people took for egotism. At this time, respectable women did not speak of themselves. Commenting on a letter in which she had written at length about herself and her children, Miss J's aunt Anna Sophia, who married the Rev. John Malleson, joked that she must have 'taken a leaf out of Miss Martineau's book as far as egotism is concerned.'[85]

The *we* form continues in HM's published writing; in *Retrospect of Western Travel*, in particular, most of her descriptions of invitations and visits are also expressed in the first person plural. In other words, after just four weeks, HM was considering Miss

J as equal to herself in experiencing America. Rather than a mere companion, Miss J had already become a trusted partner – and *witness*. As though anticipating the charge that her deafness disqualified her from writing about American society, HM took Miss J with her 'on all occasions of importance, as a witness, lest my deafness should cause mistake, or the imputation of it.'[86]

From the moment they landed at New York in mid-September 1834, the two of them were together twenty-four hours a day, seven days a week, for the next twenty months. They went as far north as the Niagara Falls and (very briefly) into Canada, south to New Orleans, and west to Chicago and Michigan, travelling over land and water by every means of transport available at the time, with unreliable drivers, uncertain companions, and unknown accommodation at the end of the day. HM had been assured 'that there will be nothing unusual or unsafe in travelling through the States with only a steady female attendant,'[87] but the very nature of their journey made it risky: horses bolt, carriages get stuck in mud, floods sweep bridges away, riverboat hulls are pierced by underwater snags, and steam locomotives invariably burst their boilers in the middle of a trestle bridge crossing a swamp. (Unlike their British counterparts, which burned coal, American steam locomotives used wood and consequently showered their passengers with smuts that burned holes in clothes and sometimes even set carriages on fire.) This was 'roughing it' indeed!

From the letter just quoted, written when HM and Miss J were near the Niagara Falls, we learn that 'we wanted to have just a peep at Ontario, as we may not live to visit it next year' – which sounds an ominous note; HM was clearly aware of the risks she was taking. She continues, 'so we went to Queenston by stage ... intending to walk back (7½ miles [12km]). We got a package of sandwiches and a bottle of cider at the inn in order to have as much time as possible for exploring.' They climbed the monu-

A 'View of the Rail-Road to Utica, taken at Little Falls' (roughly half way between Boston and Boulder) borrowed from Volume 1 of *American Scenery, with drawings W. H. Bartlett*. This railroad was chartered on 1 May 1836 (just after Miss J returned to England), and fully opened on 4 July 1839. As the book was published in 1840, this view probably dates from 1839 – possibly drawn to celebrate the opening of the line.

ment to General Brock* and viewed 'the strait, the lake, forests, villages and (alas!) battle grounds ... full of astonishment that we had heard so little of the splendid scene which lay below us.' The keeper of the monument, 'a nice little Yorkshire woman, was delighted to see countrywomen and made us eat our dinner in her cottage.' As they were resuming their walk, 'a country wagon, driven by a fine lad, passed and he asked us to let him drive us to the falls.... We were glad of such an opportunity of learning something of Canada farming, so we jumped in.'[88] In

* This is the first monument atop Queenston Heights in memory of Major General Sir Isaac Brock, killed on 13 October 1812, twenty-two years before. It had a viewing platform at the top; following an explosive attack in 1840, it was reconstructed in the 1850s, without the viewing platform.

Retrospect of Western Travel, she added, 'it was a mere box upon wheels – a barbarous machine, but of great service to us in the ensuing [rain]storm.'[89] Miss J must have shared HM's adventurous spirit, although little in her life in England can have prepared her for such spontaneous travelling as this.

The dangers they encountered were not always on the road or the river. On one occasion when they were sharing the same bed in an empty house in New Orleans – 'of all cities in the civilised world, the most renowned for night robbery and murder' – Miss J gently woke HM in the middle of the night and whispered into her ear trumpet, *'There's a man in our room.'* They had 'no light, no bell, no servants within reach ... and no idea where the slaves were to be found!' Unable to hear or see anything, HM decided to go back to sleep. Some time later, Miss J woke her again: *'He's just beside the bed!'* she whispered. Although she could see nothing in the darkness, she could hear the movements in their room. HM went back to sleep. This was repeated more than once.

'In the morning,' writes HM,

we started up to see what we had lost. My watch was safe on the table. My rings were not there; but we soon spied them rolled off to the corners of the room. The water from the baths was spilled; and our clothes were on the floor; but we missed nothing.

At breakfast Miss J managed to ascertain from the black servants that a large dog was set loose in the house at night, to deal with the rats. Her relief was great – but so had been her fear. Many years later, HM admitted that 'the moments when my companion told me that a man without shoes was walking about the room, and when, again, she heard him close by my bedside, were those of very painful fear. I have felt nothing like it on any other occasion, since I grew up.'[90]

We all feel fear when our lives are threatened; it takes courage to face that fear and move on. Quite clearly, Miss J had the guts to 'press on regardless'. Predictably, her biggest test came through HM's frank expression of her opinions.

During the first few months, HM was welcomed as a celebrity. She could go where she pleased, and proud institutions threw open their doors to show her round. The sticking point was the question of slavery. HM had made it clear, long before she left England, that she judged slavery an immoral practice that she abhorred. The Americans were forewarned, and feared the weight that her opinion could carry. She was allowed to land in New York only on the understanding that she came to *learn*, and not to *teach*.[91] Then they understood that she was also what they called an *Amalgamationist*, meaning that she saw no reason why two people who loved each other should not marry, irrespective of the colour of their skins. This was reported in all the newspapers, and the attitude towards her changed at once. All the warmth of her welcome evaporated; now she was treated coolly, with slights and even scorn.

In Philadelphia, HM was warned, *if she valued her life,* not to travel any farther south. 'At Baltimore, further obscure intimations of danger were conveyed to me: and at Washington, so many, that I felt the time was come for laying the case before my companion.' She opened their large map showing

the great extent of Southern States through which we should have to pass, probably for the most part without an escort; and always, where we were known at all, with my anti-slavery reputation uppermost in everybody's mind.

'Now, Louisa,' said I, 'does it not look awful? If you have the slightest fear, say so now, and we will change our route.'

'Not the slightest,' said she. 'If you are not afraid, I am not.'[92]

HM consoled herself with the thought that 'the murder of an English traveller would settle the business of American Slavery (in its federal sense) more speedily than perhaps any other incident.'[93] We may doubt whether Miss J was quite so sanguine about the matter.

The crisis came in Boston, fifteen months into their tour. HM and Miss J were invited to attend a meeting of the local women's Abolition Society. When HM received the invitations,

> it was impossible to have any private conversation with my companion. I therefore handed her the letters across the [dining] table, with a sign of silence; and she had five hours for reflection before the guests departed. 'Have you read those letters?' I then inquired of her. — 'Yes.' — 'Do you mean to go?' — 'Certainly, if you do.' — 'Shall I say so for you?' — 'If you please.' — I therefore accepted the invitations for both of us, and returned to the drawing-room, where I soon found an opportunity of saying to my host and hostess, 'I do not ask or wish an opinion from you: but I tell you a fact. Miss J and I are going to dine at Mr. Loring's on Wednesday, to attend an abolition meeting.' Dr. Ware turned round as he stood in the window, and said, 'You will be mobbed. You will certainly be mobbed.'[94]

Thanks to friends who accompanied them as casually as possible, they reached the door of the house where the meeting was to be held without incident. Extra precautions were nonetheless taken: the doors were locked behind them, and 'persons were stationed at the rear of the house, to keep a way clear for escape over the fence, if necessary'.

HM had come to observe, thinking that her presence was sufficient expression of her sympathy with the women's cause, but she was prevailed upon to address them, and made a brief, carefully worded statement:

> As I am requested to speak, I will say what I have said through the whole South, in every family where I have been; that I consider slavery as inconsistent with the law of God, and as incompatible with the course of his Providence. I should certainly say no less at the North than at the South concerning this utter abomination – and I now declare that in your *principles* I fully agree.[95]

This was leaked to the press, and thereafter she was insulted and threatened wherever she went for meddling with America's internal affairs. This completely changed the tenor of their visit. 'The idea of danger had become the rule, and safety the exception.'[96]

HM recalled that 'the woods of Michigan were very beautiful;' but danger was about us there, as everywhere during those three months of travel. It was out of such glades as those of Michigan that mobs had elsewhere issued to stop the coach, and demand the victim, and inflict the punishment earned by compassion for the negro, and assertion of true republican liberty. I believe there was scarcely a morning during those three months when it was not my first thought on waking whether I should be alive at night.[97]

To Miss J's role of companion was added something like that of a bodyguard, using her ears to warn of potential threats, by day and by night. She herself may not have been the target of threats, but the effect on her would have been much as if she were; she was, after all, largely responsible for HM's safety. It must have been very stressful for her.

HM intended to join a group of like-minded friends on the Ohio river (so well known to the Courtauld family), but credible news reached her of a plan in Louisville 'to hang me on the wharf before the respectable inhabitants could rescue me.' Since there were indeed frequent lynchings of Abolitionists throughout the country, she accepted that she had

less means of judging what was likely to happen than natives of the country; and [therefore] I would leave it to my own party to determine what should be done. I supposed that none of them would think of relinquishing such a scheme for mere threats; and if they were not afraid, neither was I.[98]

(Notice that she is repeating Miss J's words to her. I wonder who said them first.) The group chose to drop Louisville from their itinerary and HM lived to tell the tale.

We have to remember that throughout this time, as soon as HM was in discussion with a group of people, Miss J would be giving a running commentary in HM's speaking trumpet, so that she should miss nothing. When HM retired in the evening to record the day's events in the copious journal that she kept, Miss J would still be beside her, reporting what she had heard and seen, and confirming what had been said and decided.

In the end, though, HM decided that Miss J would have to make the return crossing to England without her. She herself remained four months longer,

> for the purpose of accompanying a party of friends to the Northern Lakes, and some new territory which it was important that I should visit. I could not afford this additional trip to more than myself; and there was not room for more than one: so my comrade preceded me homewards, sorry not to have taken that northern trip, but well satisfied with the enterprise she had achieved.[99]

Miss J sailed for England on 1st April 1836.

HM recorded that 'she was in excellent spirits up to the very last, which makes me hope that she must have more home-pleasures in prospect than I had believed.'[100] It also speaks of the degree of self-control that Miss J could command: the natural thing, when one parts from someone with whom one has shared life-threatening situations, is tears of relief. What is more, the months in America had forged a strong bond between the two women; they parted as close friends, and remained in warm and frequent contact by letter and through mutual visits for the rest of their lives.

Given the problem of 'trolling' and harassment in the world today, it is worth recalling that it could already be experienced in 1836 by a controversial figure like HM. On her return to England, she received letters from America on which she had to pay 'double, treble, even quadruple postage' (for at that time the recipient, and not the sender, paid the postage on a letter,

as a function of its weight – and it was expensive). They
    consisted mainly of envelopes, made heavy by all manner of
    devices, with a slip of newspaper in the middle, containing
    prose paragraphs, or copies of verses, full of insults, and partic-
    ularly of taunts about my deafness. All but one of these bore
    the postmark of Boston. I was ashamed to mention this back
    to America; and I hope that most of this expensive and paltry
    insult was the work of one hand.[101]
A person in HM's position is hardly better off today: they are
liable to receive personal insults and scurrilous accusations
through social media as well as the post.

‸

Safely back in England after a crossing of only twenty days, Miss
J returned to the 'home pleasures' of her former life. I believe she
went first to live in Islington with her next-to-youngest aunt,
Wilhelmina, who had married a wholesaling ironmonger,
Thomas Pickard Warren, in September 1830; he later provided
warehousing for the Courtaulds. (As already mentioned, Miss
J's grandfather, William Taylor, had had an ironmongery shop
and warehouse before he threw in his lot with the Courtauld
silk mill.) The Warrens' children had come in close succession:
John, Mary Catherine, Edward, and Sarah Wilhelmina – note
this name, for it will come back – were followed by Thomas
Pickard Warren (II) on 4 May 1837. In other words, Miss J would
have been helping her aunt with five children all under the age
of six, the youngest of whom was born just two weeks after her
return.

Quite understandably, though, she was no longer the same
person. One cannot go away for two years and experience an
entirely different life with fresh responsibilities on a different
continent, meeting famous people, facing threats of death by
violence, and come home unchanged. To start with, she clearly
had more confidence in herself. On 30 November 1836, Sarah

Bromley,* writing to Sophia Courtauld, observed, 'What a much *greater* person she is now than ever she was before she went to America with Miss Martineau. A gentleman said to me the other day at a party where Louisa was, he *supposed* Miss Jeffery would publish a book about America.'[102] If only she *had* become a Boswell to HM's Johnson! Her viewpoint would have been precious to us.

It was of course HM who published a book, *Society in America* – which she wanted to call by the much better title, *Theory and Practice of Society in America,* but her publisher thought this was too long. At the time, Miss J must have been one of the few people to know about this title change, for HM presented her with the manuscript of the book. On 25 May 1837, a few days after *Society in America* was published,† HM wrote from Westminster,

Dear Louisa,

Before starting for the country, I drop a line to tell you that your heavy mass of MS is ready for you – to be called for or forwarded, as you may direct. The papers are terribly soiled and crumpled; but you know that is done at the printing office. They will be of no *use* that I know of; but MSS are considered of value, and it is therefore that I offer these to you; whose due I feel them to be. [HM's emphasis]

---

* Sarah Bromley (born 1814) was Miss J's cousin, the daughter of her aunt Catherine who married William Bromley, legal adviser to the firm of Courtauld & Taylor. There are many letters from Sarah in the *Courtauld Family Letters*. Sarah married John Minton Courtauld, Samuel (III)'s youngest brother, and died in a riding accident in 1855. According to *The Huguenot Family of Courtauld* (volume 3, p.107) it was 'Miss MacKee' (sic) who broke the news to Samuel by letter. In 1855, Miss J was married and had a daughter who was but nine years old. The editor was surely mistaken; it would have been Mrs McKee, i.e. Miss J, who wrote the letter.

† This shows the remarkable speed with which HM wrote *Society in America:* it came out just eight months after she returned to England.

Quite clearly, the gift was not unannounced. We can be sure that HM had already spelled out her gratitude to Miss J for all her help. Short of dedicating the book to her, she chose to give the manuscript itself; *she owed it to her.* On 22 July, a somewhat awestruck Sarah Bromley reported, 'Miss Martineau has given Louisa Jeffery the MS of her book, which I suppose would be reckoned very valuable.'[103]

I do not know how long Miss J remained with the Warrens, but by the summer of 1837 she was with Kate (Mrs P. A.) Taylor. In August, Kate mentioned that 'Miss Jeffery is leaving them and does not indeed seem very well fitted for governess to great children.' To me, 'them' seems less likely to refer to the Warrens than to the Lamberts, with whom Miss J had spent much of the previous ten years and whose children were by now well into their teens and more. After her American experience, which had shown her the importance of self-discipline and self-control, Miss J may well have become less tolerant of teenage behaviour.

Kate's letter continues: 'O think, poor thing, her affair with Mr Maderson has done her no good – it has unsettled her.'[104] The 'affair with Mr Maderson' (whom I have been unable to identify) lends support to my conjecture that she had turned down a suitor in the early 1830s. (At the time, *affair* had no implication of a sexual relationship, of course.) Had it really 'unsettled her'? Or was it rather that Kate had forgotten, from her own experience of ten years before, how unsettling a visit to America could be? As it was, the genteel existence of her relatives in England must have now seemed dreadfully tame and humdrum to Miss J.

It was on 9 August 1837, when Miss J was caring for her aunt Christiana at the P. A. Taylors', that Kate exclaimed that Miss J 'would be a treasure to many a one.'[105] Her aunt's headache at this time may not be unrelated to the declining health of their old Aunt P, who died a month later; both Miss J and Christiana were present when she expired. In July a year later, HM mentioned to an American friend that 'Miss Jeffery is quite well, and always useful in an extensive family circle, though she has no very near relations.'[106]

Did Christiana manage to express how much she appreciated Miss J's care and support, and persuade her to return to the Lamberts' at Banstead? She was certainly living with them in the autumn of 1839 when HM collapsed while travelling on the Continent from the effects of what turned out to be an ovarian cyst. (By the time she died in 1876, it had grown to a massive volume of about six litres.[107]) She was repatriated to the home of her uncle in Newcastle. Miss J offered to send her a pair of slippers as a memento of their time together. Answering on 2 November 1839, HM told her that she would be 'particularly thankful' for the slippers, 'now that I cannot warm my feet by exercise.' On the other hand, she did not need anything to remind her of Miss J, for 'I have my own feelings to remind me of you. I owe you too much ever to forget you.'[108] She added that Miss J might borrow whatever books she wished from her library in London. Now that's a sign of how deeply she trusted Miss J; I know of no other instance of HM allowing someone to make free use of her library – in her absence, furthermore.

In April the following year, Miss J offered 'to companionize or nurse' HM if required, but HM, independent as ever, declined 'even so great and kind a service,' adding, 'such illness as I have is best borne alone.... I am equal to writing *if I have no other call upon my strength.*' She preferred to be alone and do as she pleased, 'without the effort of *listening* – the fatigue of which to me, you know of old.'[109] Rarely did HM acknowledge this problem (just as she rarely used emphases like these in her letters).

❦

Ever since her schooldays, Miss J had maintained her friendship with Mary Beard, who had ten children, only five of whom survived to adulthood. Aided by an assistant, John Relly Beard taught his own children, boys and girls alike, in the school that he set up in his home to supplement his meagre stipend (much as Miss J's father had done). He gave his daughter Sarah (1831–1922) the same lessons that her eldest brother Charles (born four years earlier) had had. 'My father had quite modern notions about female education,' she recalled with dry understatement, 'and was very desirous of making me an independent woman, with a career of my own. All his plans were defeated by my early engagement and marriage' – of which more in due course.[110] His educational method was based on principles derived from 'Froebel and Pestalozzi – even from Rousseau;' a contemporary compared Beard with Dr Arnold of Rugby.[111] McLachlan's *Records of a Family* lists a number of his pupils who made their mark thanks to his teaching, and his own offspring, and their children, became 'pioneers in education, social service and liberal education' (to borrow the subtitle of McLachlan's book). When Sarah was still a schoolgirl, a doctor's wife made a telling observation about her family. 'My dear,' she said, 'there are three aristocracies: one of birth, one of wealth, and one of talent. Your family belongs to the aristocracy of talent.'[112] In retrospect, it seems quite perceptive.

By 1833, the success of Beard's school justified the building of a house large enough to accommodate boarders as well as day boys alongside his family, and he equipped it with 'a library, a large playground, scientific apparatus, a gymnasium, and garden plots for cultivation by the boys.... Mrs Beard ... had charge of the domestic arrangements.'[113] Although there is no record of when, or how frequently, Miss J visited the Beards, she was surely with them during some of her absences from the Taylor-Courtauld family circle. As Mary Beard was running a small boarding school at the same time as looking after her own growing family, we can be sure that she greatly appreciated the help that Miss J could give during her visits.

The principal teacher that Beard employed – for ten years – was the Rev. James Riddell McKee (born in Drumbo, County

Down, in 1805); living in the Beards' house, he participated in their family life. Sarah Beard recorded in 1912 that McKee 'made a great pet of me when I was a little girl and, for his sake, I have always loved Irishmen.'[114] On Miss J's visits, she too came to love James McKee, whose marriage proposal she accepted in 1842. Telling HM of her engagement, she anticipated disapproval, knowing her negative opinion of late marriages. At once, HM, who was still confined to her room at Tynemouth, wrote back a long chatty letter to reassure her:

> I have always wished to see you married, – as much from my very high opinion of your domestic qualities and eminent womanly virtues as from my belief of the necessity of a strong attachment to your happiness; and I therefore hear of this engagement with great satisfaction.[115]

HM cannot have known that, almost forty years before, Miss J's mother had been described in very similar terms: 'endowed with ... a kind and affectionate disposition, and a mind in every respect calculated to promote and insure domestic felicity.' This suggests that the obituary notice of 1808 had not been just gilding the lily. HM ended her letter with 'every good wish and strong interest in your happiness.'[116]

Naturally, Miss J informed her relatives of her forthcoming marriage. Her uncle Samuel Courtauld (III) reacted promptly. He and Ellen had lost their first (and ultimately only) child, named Ellen Taylor Courtauld, in August 1841, shortly before her second birthday, so he was especially sensitive to the fate of parentless children like Miss J. By the time of the 1851 census, Samuel had informally adopted two girls: the first was Sarah Ann Cawston, born in 1840, whose father had died when she was one. Then his wife had taken pity on Louisa Harris, born in November 1844, whose mother had died when she was two weeks old. In the 1871 census, he also listed Emily Ely, born around 1817, as an 'adopted daughter', but she was not treated as such in his Will. Quite unrelated to the Taylor and Courtauld families, she seems to have spent her life being useful to them, rather as Miss J had been doing. My guess is that Samuel made some kind of settlement on Miss J prior to her marriage, probably to ensure her independence in the case of widowhood, and possibly to ensure a good education for any children (or perhaps just daughters) that she might have.

In confidence, Miss J sent a copy of the settlement – if that is the right name for it – to HM for her comments; she responded in September 1843:

I hope you have not been uneasy about your precious papers. My delay has been owing to anything but carelessness, or want of interest, as you shall see.

This confidence of yours has the effect which, I fully believe, every revelation of your mind would have, – of confirming my respect and regard for you. I congratulate you on the issue, but in my heart I congratulate you much more on the scrupulous integrity of Mr C's admirable kindness to you. I am delighted at his generosity: and the whole affair is one which warms one's heart and helps one's faith. In saying this, do I not best thank you for your confidence?

Now – I have something to say which I will speak straight out in the same reliance upon your sincerity and your good constructions as of old. – I see you really would like to be by my side again, before you go off to a new home, and the duties of a life [sic, for *wife*].

... Now, how would you like to come (wholly at my expense) about the 1st of October, and at all events spend a fortnight with me; and, if Maria stays, a month?... [You could] spend the evenings with me, and you and I could have plentiful tete-a-tetes in the mornings.

If you come, how much we shall have to say! It would give me great pleasure.

And an afterthought: If it suits you better to come any sooner than October 1st, pray do so.[117]

I have made this a lengthy quotation because it tells us so much about HM's warm relationship with Miss J, her respect for her and pleasure she took in her company. It tells us rather less about the precise nature of Samuel Courtauld's generosity.

Miss J and James McKee were married at Newington Green* (now subsumed in north London), on 2 January 1844.[118] From there, they went to live in Devon, where McKee 'had taken the headmastership of a new proprietary school at Tavistock, established for the sons of the gentry and tradesmen of the town and neighbourhood.'[119] Their first child, a girl, was born on 26 November that same year and named Ellen Courtauld McKee, after Miss J's aunt and the child she had lost. Six years later, on 24 December 1850, they had a son, whom they named Samuel Jeffery McKee, combining her generous uncle's first name with Miss J's maiden name.

In January 1845, a year after she married, Miss J received a light-hearted message from Charles, the eldest of the Beards' sons; he was just beginning the divinity studies that were to make him a friend and then colleague of James Martineau. 'Your humble servant is just as he was,' he wrote, 'only decidedly more sober, works harder, and has taken an immense liking to metaphysics, and (*don't tell Mr McKee*) hates mathematics worse than ever.'[120] This shows the degree of trust and affection between the McKees and the Beard children that Mr McKee had helped to educate; it developed into 'a lasting family friendship.' One thing surprises me: although the eldest Beard daughter, Sarah, remembered Miss J as 'a very interesting woman' in the recollections she recorded in 1912,[121] none of her family seems to have recalled (in print, at any rate) hearing Miss J tell of her visit to America and the adventures that she and HM had shared. They would surely have kept the children – and their parents – spellbound.

---

*   Newington Green being the home of English Dissenters, their wedding was probably celebrated in the Unitarian church there.

At this time, Miss J helped to bring about a previously unrecorded episode in HM's life. Laid low by her ovarian cyst, HM lay in a chaise longue at Tynemouth and nursed her discomfort in privacy and seclusion for five years, while intermittently writing. Her *Life in the Sick-room* (1843) was seized upon by Georgiana Bell* and, as she put it to Sophia, devoured 'with delight'.[122] In June 1844, having found no other way to relieve her condition, HM called in a man who practised mesmerism, a forerunner of hypnotism. He proved unable to mesmerize her, but after he had left, HM and her maid discovered that they could do it to each other perfectly well, and within a few weeks HM felt well enough to return to her previous active life, travelling and writing. In fact, she seems to have been even more physically active after this immobilization than before it: in January 1845 she embarked on a nine-month trip to Egypt and Palestine that involved much riding around on horses, donkeys, and camels. Three years later, she was in Fleetwood for a month, 'to bathe and run by the sea when not writing.'[123]

When HM brought out *Letters on Mesmerism* late in 1845, its readers were sharply divided into those who believed in its efficacy and those who dismissed it as charlatanism – or even the work of the devil. Sophia Courtauld read it and it gave her hopes: her eyesight had long been poor, and now she was going deaf; in

---

* A footnote in Volume 4 of the *Courtauld Family Letters* informs us that 'Mrs Bell was only a distant relative [of the Courtaulds]: her sister, Mrs Jameson, was a Miss Cornelia Campion, related to Mrs George Courtauld's mother, who was a Miss Eliza Williamson before she became Stephen Minton's second wife.' I shall leave the reader to fathom that one out, and add only that she was married to a Mr Edward Bell and put either 'Richmond' or 'Poet's Corner' at the head of her letters. She and her husband were distant friends of HM. In a PS to a letter to Sophia, postmarked 11 August 1847, HM wrote that 'Mrs Ed. Bell looks very well, and is coming to spend an evening here, as are the Sydney Bells' (*Courtauld Family Letters*, Vol. 7, p.3248).

fact, there was 'so much the matter with her' (as HM put it to Miss J) that she was clutching at straws. She asked Kate (Mrs P. A.) Taylor to ask Miss J if she would ask HM to use mesmerism to cure her deafness (quite overlooking the fact that HM had not been cured of her own deafness by this means).[124] Miss J wrote as requested and, despite her extraordinarily busy life, HM responded favourably, saying that she would be 'most happy to mesmerize Miss C' and give 'her best attention' to Sophia's case. She did, however, add very honestly that 'I cannot say I have any hope about the deafness.'[125]

In April 1846, Sophia, accompanied by William Fox's daughter Eliza, who was keen to see HM again, travelled up to the Lake District, where HM had just moved into the house she had built for herself in Ambleside, The Knoll.* Soon after, Samuel Courtauld reported to his brother George that the ladies were 'most kindly received by Miss Martineau, whose first mesmeriz-ings seem beneficial,'[126] but a letter from HM to Sophia shows that she had not been successful. 'We go on but badly,' it begins, 'but I cannot help it. I feel that I have overdone the matter and must omit mesmerizing, at least for some days.... I don't think you are a subject for mesmerizing.' She ended by sending her 'love to Miss Fox.'[127]

Two years later, in the summer of 1847, Sophia sent HM a brooch as a thank-you present. In her grateful reply HM said that she had been pleased to learn, from Mr and Mrs P. A. Taylor, that Sophia 'had derived *some* benefit from further mesmerizing; though I fear it was not much.'[128] A year later, Sophia was in the north again, at Ben Rhydding, in Yorkshire, where there was a newly opened hydropathic establishment. HM walked over to it from 'Laund House' (which apparently no longer exists, al-though the farmhouse does) on what is now the Bolton Abbey Estate: a matter of about eight miles (more than 12km) in each

---

* Coincidentally, the Beards' family home was called 'Stony Knolls'.

direction. I do not know if they practised mesmerism on this occasion, but they certainly parted on very friendly terms, with HM sending 'love to K.T.'[129] (The initials designate Kate (Mrs P. A.) Taylor's daughter Catherine Taylor (II), known as Katie, born in June 1829, who was accompanying Sophia on this occasion.) As a result of these contacts with the Courtaulds, HM held the family in high esteem.

Miss J's married life continued with a move up north, to Pendleton – not far from the Beards' – some time before the birth of Samuel in December 1850. I am not sure quite why they left Tavistock. It may be that Mr McKee hoped to make more money with a school of his own. It can hardly have been for his health: in December 1845, HM told her friend Sarah Wetmore Story, whom she and Miss J had met and liked during their visit to America, that 'he is an excellent man; and nothing would be wanting to Louisa's happiness if he were but strong enough to do all that he would wish, for her sake, – to increase their small means.'[130] HM reverted to his health in a letter to Sophia, two years later, saying that she feared that he was 'very delicate'.[131] At this point, he had only just turned forty, and he was seventy-eight when he died, which suggests that he looked after himself very well – or was it not rather Miss J, who had cared for HM 'like a mother' in America, who looked after him so well?

After Tavistock, down in Devon, Pendleton (now part of Salford, Greater Manchester) must have seemed like something out of Dante's Inferno: it was a small country village rapidly turning into a sprawling semi-industrial suburb, with terraced houses among coal mines and cotton mills. It instantly became overcrowded and insanitary – and took a hundred-and-fifty years to clean up. There the McKees opened another school, to which the Beards sent their youngest son, James Rait Beard, in 1853. But he was with them for only a year: in the middle of 1854, the McKees moved back southwards, to Shrewsbury. Again, I do not know what motivated the move; but when the opportunity arose, they hastened to grasp it. In complete contrast to Pendleton, Shrewsbury is a market town not far from the border with Wales; it has a medieval street plan that is largely unchanged even today, with hundreds of beautiful buildings, including several with timber frames from the fifteenth and sixteenth centuries. The McKees lived on Claremont Hill, in the old town centre, close to the Unitarian chapel* of which McKee was the incumbent until he retired nineteen years later. Around 1880, they joined their children in London.

WHEN I BEGAN RESEARCHING the life of Miss J, I thought that this was where my account would end, with the McKees happily married, raising two delightful children, fondly remembered by the Courtaulds, the Taylors, the Beards, and HM. But Miss J's daughter had more in store for me: I came across mentions of Ellen McKee in studies of how women strove, in the second half of the nineteenth century, to obtain the right to vote and (more successfully) the right to elect and be elected to local district councils, school boards, and Poor-Law boards. In *Women, Educational Policy-Making and Administration in England: Authoritative Women Since 1800*, Professor Jane Martin mentions the work of many activists, including Ellen McKee, who, she writes, 'emerged from an obscure background,' adding

* Charles Darwin's mother, Susannah, the granddaughter of Josiah Wedgwood (one of the founder members of the Unitarian movement), regularly attended this chapel, as did Charles, until her death in 1817. Then, at the age of eight, he joined his brother in a nearby Anglican school.

that 'nothing is known of her lifestyle.'[132] Having thrown some light on her background, I decided to reveal what I could of her life, if not exactly its style. In doing so, I discovered how close she was to HM, to Samuel Courtauld's adopted daughter Sarah Ann Cawston, and also to Sarah Beard and her daughter Mary. It also enables me to complete the life of Miss J.

After she married, Miss J remained in regular contact with HM, who destroyed letters as fast as she received them, so none of Miss J's letters to her have survived. Nor did Miss J save many of HM's letters. An indication, however, of the quality of their exchanges can be gauged by a letter from HM to William Story, who was preparing a life of his father, Joseph Story, Associate Justice of the Supreme Court of the United States. (He was one of the many prominent people that HM and Miss J had met in America, and with whom she corresponded after she returned to England.) In 1846, in preparation for his biography, William Story asked HM to send back him any letters that his father might have written to her. She hastened to do so, adding in her answer that she had passed one of the letters on to Miss J, and that she had asked Miss J to return it to him.[133] So HM was sharing with Miss J some of the personal letters that she received.

Among the few letters from HM to Miss J that have survived, one from 1854 invites Miss J to come and stay, bringing her husband and children. HM assured her, 'I have room for you all four: and if you don't know what to do with a maid, bring her too.'[134] In the early 1850s, HM invited herself to stay with the McKees for three nights. 'I am reckoning much on my visit to you and yours, dear Louisa,' she wrote.* 'All I ask is that you will not put yourselves out of the way on my account, but remember that I am perfectly well in health, and a hardened old traveller who can sleep anywhere'[135] – and (we might add) at any time,

---

* Logan could not date this letter. I calculate it to have been December 1853, since HM refers to the upcoming 'Monday 2ⁿᵈ January'. At this time, 1854 was the only year in which when the second of January fell on a Monday.

even when she believed that a man was standing right beside her bed! As HM recalled, it was still 'pleasant to talk over our American adventures in her house or in mine.'[136]

In this free and easy friendship – by Victorian standards, at any rate – HM was quite open with Miss J about her health: '*You* have a title to know something of how I am,' she had written back in 1839.[137] In the mid-1850s, when she was very unwell and her doctor feared that she might not have long to live, she revealed more physical details to Miss J than to other correspondents. In a letter dated May 1855, when she was writing her autobiography,* she detailed how she was feeling and added, almost as an afterthought,

> It has often occurred to me to ask whether you have any plan
> for your mid-summer holidays. It is a long way off yet; and all
> manner of things may be in the way; and asking the question
> may be a great liberty, but yet, you see, I do it.[138]

Miss J mistook this as an indirect request for her to come and help as a 'nurse or assistant nurse.'[139] HM hastened to assure her that she had been thinking rather of

> the pleasure of your company as a guest – but then, I do not see
> what right I have to do so, considering how very little I am able
> to converse or listen.... Let me just say this:– that if it is likely
> to be at all convenient and pleasure to you to come and spend
> a fortnight with M[ary] and me, in the fairest season of the
> valley and will put up with such a reception as we may be able
> to offer you, it will give me *great* pleasure to have you.

---

* Although HM did not want her *Autobiography* to be published before her death, she had it printed, so that her Executor should have 'no responsibility, & scarcely any trouble' with it (*Chapman*, p.475). She sent Miss J an offprint of one of the portraits of herself that appear in the book, and was 'so glad' that she liked it. 'It is a painful thing to have one which one does *not* think like.' In *Collected Letters,* Logan adds '[sic]' after the *like*; quite clearly, she does not understand British English: here *like* still means *a good likeness*, a hundred-and-sixty years later.

Plainly speaking, my state prevents my asking any gentleman to the house,– any guest but one womanly friend with
whom I may take my freedom. *You* would have *your* freedom,
abundantly.[140]

In this strong attachment to Miss J, HM reveals how much she
appreciated Miss J's company – and possibly the mothering that
her own mother had failed to provide – at the same time as her
respect for other people: however much she wanted Miss J to
come and stay, she refused to order her around or *use* her.

In October 1854, she expressed her pleasure at finally meeting
Miss J's uncle Samuel Courtauld (III). This came about through
his and HM's efforts to prevent the *Westminster Review* (with
Marian Evans, better known by her pseudonym George Eliot, as
its assistant editor) from falling into unsuitable hands. 'I will
only say that this close intercourse with Mr Courtauld has raised
my respect for him to the highest possible point,' she exclaimed.

I before respected him as much as I could anyone whom I knew
only by the affectionate report of three or four people: but now
there have been so many evidences of goodness, moral and
intellectual – in short, of *wisdom*.

She goes on to report hearing a lawyer declare, 'What a clear-
headed man this is!' So it was with genuine pleasure that she
announced, 'I have a kind invitation to visit Mr and Mrs C at
either Bocking or Brighton;* and they have promised to come to
me – we hope next year.'[141] (I am not aware that either of these
visits ever took place.)

From HM's letters to Miss J, it would appear that Ellen was
not schooled locally, nor educated at home by her parents,
but sent elsewhere. For instance, when her brother Samuel was
born on 24 December 1850, HM – no doubt remembering the

---

* Bocking is the nearest village to Folley House; Brighton is where the
Courtaulds, or at least Samuel, for his wife did not enjoy travelling, often
stayed in the summer with Miss J's aunt, Anna Sophia Taylor, who had
married the Rev. John Philip Malleson – or rented a house nearby.

emotional impact of the birth of her own little brother James –
wrote, 'What a prodigious event it will be to her, *when she comes
home.*'[142] It could be that Ellen was simply staying with a relative,
kept out of the way for the birth, but when the 1851 census was
taken three months later, she was still not at home; instead she
was at Blendon Hall, in Kent.* In the same household were
Louisa Harris and Sarah Ann Cawston, along with Emily Ely
as their governess. So it looks very much as though Ellen was
educated (if only in part) alongside Samuel Courtauld's adopted
daughters. (He clearly liked Blendon Hall: he rented it for six
months in 1851, but in 1854 he acquired Gosfield Hall† instead.)
This supports my hypothesis that the settlement he made prior
to Miss J's marriage provided for the education of (at least) her
daughter. Ellen certainly became good friends with Sarah Ann
Cawston, as we shall see in due course.

Ellen's education away from home continued in the 1850s. In
March 1853, when HM was hoping for a visit from the McKees,
she wrote, 'Nelly [the familiar diminutive of *Ellen*] will be with
you then, I suppose. I have room for you all four.' She ended the
letter with her love to Sam and Nelly 'when you write,' which
means that Miss J was communicating with both her children by
letter.[143] Soon Ellen herself began writing to HM.

* Blendon Hall was the home of Oswald Smith (1794–1863), a banker. Two
  years after the 1851 census was taken, his daughter Frances Dora married
  Claude Bowes-Lyon; Queen Elizabeth II is her great granddaughter.

† Built in 1545, Gosfield Hall had strong links with past royalty: it hosted
  royal visits by Queen Elizabeth I and her retinue throughout the middle of
  the sixteenth century. At the beginning of the eighteenth, its Grand Salon
  was reconstructed and for a long time it served as the State banqueting
  hall. Fleeing the French Revolution, Louis XVIII and Marie-Joséphine
  of Savoy lived in Gosfield Hall from 1807 to 1809 with their 350 courtiers
  and staff. Samuel Courtauld spent a lot of money restoring it. What a place
  for Miss J and her family to visit! After Courtauld's death, his adopted
  daughter Louisa Lowe (née Harris) lived there, but in the twentieth century
  it fell into disrepair and was used to house soldiers during WWII.

Even though the mid-1850s were among the busiest years in HM's life – she wrote her autobiography at the same time as contributing no less than 1600 articles to the *Daily News* alone, sometimes writing as many as six leaders a week – she still found time to acknowledge the presents and letters she received from little Ellen. In September 1853, for instance, she thanked her (using her pet name 'Nelly') for a book marker. HM found it 'very pretty', adding: 'I once had one given me, but it is very much broken and faded; and now I shall begin directly to use yours. You may be sure I shall not "forget" you.' (It surely depicted forget-me-nots – probably embroidered with them. Needlework of this kind was a typical exercise for little girls – and HM herself was as adept with her needle as she was with her pen.) She invited Ellen to come and visit her again, bringing her brother Sam: 'We'll see what he will say to the little ducks and chicks, now that he can talk....The cows are very well thank you; and we make very fine butter now.'[144] HM, the distinguished political commentator and author, could also write to a little girl – Ellen was not quite eight at this point – without condescension and with obvious affection. In fact, she seems to have played the role of honorary aunt to Ellen, filling a gap in her family circle.

As the letters, presents and visits continued, Ellen grew up into a young lady with her own mind and political awareness – very much a modern woman. In this we may see the influence of HM, who (we should not forget) was 'one of the women – perhaps the first among them – who made the nineteenth century the dawn of freedom for half the human race.'[145] In the chapter on the 'Political non-Existence of Women' in *Society in America*, HM had shown how discrimination and disregard for the rights of women placed them on a level equivalent to that of slaves.[146] And writing in the *Edinburgh Magazine* in April 1859, she argued that it was logical that women should have a right to equal pay for equal work, to mention only the most striking of her conclusions. Close association with such an advocate for women could hardly fail to make an impression upon Ellen.

Nor was HM the only political influence on her. Miss J's cousin, Peter Alfred Taylor (II), had joined the family firm of Courtauld & Taylor as soon as he was of age, becoming a partner in 1849, but his heart was not in it. He soon cashed in his share and devoted the rest of his life to his main interest, politics, becoming the MP for Leicester in 1861. According to the *Dictionary of National Biography,*

> In home politics Taylor was an advanced radical, and in his persistent opposition to government extravagance and social inequalities of the pettier kind he may be regarded as the chief custodian for his time of the political principles of the Manchester school. In every English movement for the promotion of freedom he took a keen interest, and generally occupied an official position.[147]

In the House of Commons, Taylor worked closely with John Stuart Mill and Henry Fawcett* in supporting the idea of giving women the right to vote. His wife Mentia (née Clementia Doughty, whom he had met at the home and school of his uncle John Philip Malleson down in Brighton) assembled the 1521 signatures of the 1866 Women's Suffrage Petition for John Stuart Mill to lay before the House on 7 June 1866. Mill declared that the petition had been organized and signed exclusively by women; thus it clearly demonstrated for the first time that women wanted the vote. The names of Miss J and Ellen McKee (still only twenty at that point) were on the list, as was HM's, and Sophia Courtauld's. Taylor presented further petitions from Shrewsbury in 1869 and 1870. By 1871, there was a suffrage committee in Shrewsbury, with Miss J as president and Ellen as secretary. When the census was taken on 2 April that year, Ellen was staying with Peter and Mentia Taylor in London.

---

* Henry Fawcett (1833–84) was the author of a *Manual of Political Economy* (1863) – he was of course known to HM. More of him later.

Beside militating in favour of women (for which she has been dubbed 'the mother' of the parliamentary suffrage movement), Mentia was a leader of the anti-slavery campaign in England; she founded the Ladies' London Emancipation Society, of which HM was of course a member. Ellen joined it too; some time later, she also became a member of the London National Society for Women's Suffrage, whose secretary was Mentia. After Peter Alfred Taylor (II) bought Aubrey House in Holland Park, London, in 1863, he and Mentia created the Aubrey Institute,* which became a focal point for radical political leaders, including Italians like Mazzini and Garibaldi. In the suffrage campaign, it supported women's efforts to obtain seats on local school boards. They got their foot in the door, so to speak, when Parliament allowed that, with respect to membership of the school boards created under the 1870 Education Act, words denoting *men* could also be construed to include *women*. At last, women were to get a voice in the education of their children. Until then, all decisions about teachers and pupils in schools had been taken by all-male committees. But it was one thing to have a right: it was quite another to persuade men to let them exercise that right. Very few women achieved it before the twentieth century. One of them was Ellen.

In the meantime, she and her mother were still in regular contact with HM, whose steadily declining physical condition left her able to do little beyond hauling herself from her bed to a couch and back again, but whose affection for them remained as strong as ever. She was 'always glad to hear of you and yours,' as she put it to Miss J on 2 November 1871,[48] and just as desirous of their company. Sometimes, HM's sisters Ellen Higginson or Rachel Martineau, or her niece Jane (who in 1864 took over from Maria as HM's nurse) would write to Miss J, discussing the diffi-

---

* Just as Miss J had contributed her memories to P. A. Taylor (II)'s book about the Taylor family, so Ellen contributed her memories of this time to F. M. Gladstone's 1922 book about Aubrey House.

culties of caring for HM and thanking Miss J for all her help, advice, and loving attention. As in the Courtauld letters, she was universally appreciated.

HM enjoyed Ellen's visits too. Planning to receive her from 30 December 1872, she wrote,

> If a fortnight must be the limit of your stay, we* shall be thankful to you for giving us what you can. But if you can stay longer, our obligation will be all the greater: and we leave this point to your kindness – if you in fact have any more time at your command....
>
> We feel we are asking a great favour in proposing this visit from you.[149]

HM, whose acquaintance had been sought by presidents and princes, was reduced to seeking 'the favour' of a visit from the twenty-eight-year-old Ellen. She was uncomfortably aware that she could no longer be good company for visitors, least of all someone of Ellen's age, but she really wanted her to come. She was no doubt keen to have news of her activities in London and to encourage her on the arduous path towards exercising her political rights as a woman.

Three years later, after HM had declined Miss J's offer to come and help out in a domestic crisis, Ellen volunteered to come and stay for a month. HM was extremely grateful. Her two main needs, she explained, were, firstly, the writing of letters. They could be 'as short as you please, while serving as bulletins to my family and dear friends. These letters, and such as are required by business, form the most prominent service which you can render me,' for she was finding it increasingly difficult to hold a pen. The second service was 'simply your presence in the house.... There must be someone at the head of the house to be applied to.'[150] 'I shall ask for all you can tell me of my dear old friend Mr Courtauld,' she added.[151] Ellen came and stayed as

---

* This is not a royal we: HM is including Jane, her nurse and companion.

planned, but from subsequent letters to her from HM, it is clear that Ambleside was too quiet for her: she missed the excitement of London life and politics.

Judging by the letters that survive, their correspondence continued until close to the end of 1875. In September that year, HM acknowledged another letter from Ellen, deplored her declining health, exclaimed over household matters – 'the preserves this year are prodigious!' – and expressed how pleased she was that Ellen had been to France 'and seen *some* of the beauties of poor Paris. I wish the Commune had let you see them all first.'[152] The last letter we have ends with, 'Goodbye, dear Ellen! My love to your Mother, and kind regards to your father and brother.'[153] HM died on 27 June, 1876. Miss J was among the very first to be informed.

The older generation were passing on: Samuel Courtauld died in March 1881, leaving his 'daughters' Sarah Ann Cawston and Louisa Harris the bulk of his fortune: trust funds endowed with £70,000 and £80,000 respectively, plus a house and an estate each. Emily Ely, on the other hand, received only £5000. Ellen's brother Sam, who was one of the executors of Courtauld's Will, also received £5000, while Ellen and her mother got only £2000 each. In this difference of treatment I see confirmation that they had already benefitted from his generosity. It may even have been spelled out in the settlement made shortly before Miss J married, so that his bequests contained no surprises for them.

Ellen's father, James McKee, died in August 1883, and Miss J followed him in September 1887. She left an estate of £2952 to be shared by Ellen and Sam. By this time, Sam had become a solicitor; having done his articles in Shrewsbury, he had joined the firm of Jason, Cobb, Pearson & Co. in London. He also served as legal adviser to various women's associations, including the Society for Promoting the Return (i.e. election) of Women as Poor-Law Guardians, of which Ellen was a founding member in 1888. Once he was settled in London, he and Ellen lived together

on a modest footing; they clearly saw eye-to-eye when it came
to empowering women.

I have found no record of their social lives, but there is one
family they surely got to know, if only distantly: the famous
Garrett girls, Elizabeth (1836–1917) and Millicent (1847–1929) –
to mention only two of them – and their youngest brother Sam.
Just like Ellen's brother, Sam Garrett was born in 1850 and
became a London solicitor. He is noted for his support of his
sisters' campaigns: Elizabeth pioneered in opening the medical
profession to women and created the first Hospital for Women,
which Ellen supported with donations from its foundation in
1872; in 1909 she was made a life governor of it. Millicent Garrett,
whose life overlapped with Ellen's from start to finish, is an icon
of the women's rights movement. She and Ellen championed the
same causes, including the access of women to school boards,
and were members of the same associations, starting with the
London Society for Women's Suffrage. Both were active in what
became the National Union of Women's Suffrage Societies
(NUWSS), rather than the militant Women's Social and Political
Union (WSPU); in other words, they were suffra*gists* rather than
suffra*gettes*. Nor should we forget that Millicent was the author
of *Political Economy for Beginners* (1870), which must have
endeared her to those close to HM. She married Henry Fawcett
(1833–1884), whom we have already noticed as the MP who
worked with Peter Alfred Taylor (II). (Fawcett lost his sight in a
shooting accident in 1858; this did not prevent him from leading
an active life in politics and as a professor at Cambridge.) It was
at Aubrey House that Millicent and Henry Fawcett first met,
when she was not quite eighteen. He overheard her confidently
express an independent opinion, which was still considered
unladylike, especially in one so young. This so struck him that
he asked Mentia to introduce them. They were married before
Millicent was twenty.

For all her feminist activities, I do not know how Ellen filled her days between 1866 and 1886. She *may* have visited America in 1879: a passenger named Ellen C. McKee is recorded as sailing directly to Philadelphia in that year. By this time, however, Louisa Perina Courtauld (II) had returned to England, and all three of the Courtauld-Wharton girls mentioned earlier, Louisa, Amelia and Sarah, had died without issue, so there would have been no blood relatives over there for her to visit. On the other hand, she may simply have wanted to see for herself the society that she must have heard so much about from her mother and HM.

In 1886, Ellen managed to get herself elected as a Poor-Law Guardian for Marylebone. The Board of Poor-Law Guardians oversaw the running of the parish workhouse and met once a week to examine applications for relief – food, clothing, and a little money – or entry into the workhouse. Ellen was also an early member (alongside Millicent Garrett) of the Women's Local Government Society, founded in 1888 as the Society for Promoting the Return of Women as County Councillors. It aimed to increase the number of women seeking elected office and, concomitantly, to increase the number of women entitled to vote in local government elections. She served on its executive in the 1890s. At about this time, she was also Chairman of Managers of the Kentish Town Group of Board Schools, and in this capacity she gave evidence to a Departmental Committee Inquiring into the Poor Law Schools. She went on record for affirming that it was pointless to feed the mind of a child if its body was not properly fed: the only thing a hungry child will learn is how and where to find food.[154] Then in 1897 she gained a seat on the London School Board (LSB), which at the time was the largest organ of local government in Britain, second only to Parliament in its power, 'if power be measured by influence for good or evil over masses of human beings,' as *The Times* put it in 1870.[155] Established under the 1870 Education Act, the LSB was one of the first public bodies in England to admit women on the same terms as men. In the first election, Elizabeth Garrett MD won the poll in Marylebone with 47,858 votes; Professor Thomas Huxley came second with 13,494. It was a triumph that was never repeated.

It was far harder for women to gain access to the LSB than it was for men. The Board comprised fifty-one members, elected through a process very similar to a parliamentary election, with a campaign, canvassing, hustings, and so forth; fresh elections were held every three years. For many men, membership of the Board served as a stepping-stone to Parliament; for women, it could only be an end in itself, expressing their desire to improve the education and conditions of London's teeming children. Consequently, during the thirty years of its existence, a total of only twenty-nine women won seats on the Board, there being never more than ten of them serving at any one time, and sometimes as few as two. Writing in the mid-1980s, Patricia Hollis (aka Baroness Hollis of Heigham) wrote feelingly about the personal qualities required of these women:

> Knowing how much courage it takes even now for many women to stand for election, make public speeches, and chair local authority committees; and appreciating how much harder it was then for women to affront social proprieties and male sensibilities, I would claim for those elected women moral courage of a high order. It takes nerve and fortitude to smash windows and endure hunger-striking as the suffragettes did; it also takes considerable courage to impose yourself on a board when your presence is deeply resented, and to offer service of a most personally demanding kind, year in and year out. Hard perhaps for men, in their overwhelming majorities and taking for granted the camaraderie of work and politics, to realize the bravery required of women who were isolated from any party or sisterly support.[156]

Male resistance to letting women play any part in the administration of institutions can be illustrated by the Board of

Management of the Royal Hospital for Incurables at Putney Heath. Having rejected the idea that women should be admitted to the Board for almost thirty years, they were faced in 1893 with a recommendation for their admission by Lord Aberdeen, in his capacity as Chairman of a Commission of Inquiry into the affairs of the Hospital. They did not react until the Annual Meeting in 1897, when a motion on the subject was tabled for discussion, after which they hastily appointed a committee of lady visitors. As the 1898 Meeting approached, they argued, in a circular sent to subscribers, that the existence of lady visitors rendered superfluous the admission of women to the Board. At the Meeting, they claimed that 'ladies were incompetent to deal with large sums of money' – completely ignoring the fact that women on the LSB administered far larger sums than they ever had to handle. They also protested that 'there would be an awkwardness in discussing physical ailments in a mixed committee.'[157] This all-male Board felt no awkwardness about discussing intimate details of the inmates of the Hospital, eighty percent of whom were women, cared for by a large staff of female nurses and servants. Ellen spoke for the resolution on behalf of the LSB, but the motion to admit women to the Board of Management was rejected once again.

It was no sinecure to be on the London School Board:

As a minimum, a member of the LSB would attend the public sitting of the Board every Wednesday afternoon during session, as well as fortnightly meetings of two other committees and two or three sub-committees. Indeed, there is evidence that members spent two or three days a week at the Board offices on the Embankment, while constituency work made further inroads into their time: a heavy burden in a period when elected officials were not entitled to draw out-of-pocket expenses or recoup lost earnings.[158]

I have emphasized the first three words of this quotation, for conscientious Board members could find themselves working

far harder. What is more, they were not paid, so they often dug
deep into their own pockets to help provide for the children and
schools they supervised. To do this, they needed a solid private
income, or outside funding – or both. Rosamund Davenport Hill
spent £1,500 on her early contests; after that, 'Rothschild picked
up the bills.'[159] Over a two-year period, 1880–82, Miss Hill
attended a record 634 committee meetings,[160] becoming 'an
acknowledged expert on the industrial training of unruly girls.'[161]
Ellen took over Miss Hill's City seat on the Board, and she
presided the Industrial Schools Committee, 'avidly support[ing]
the domestic curriculum that her predecessor had helped to
expand.'[162]

Did Ellen meet all her costs out of her own pocket? As we
have seen, she had inherited some money during the 1880s:
£2000 from Samuel Courtauld; less than £1500 from her
parents, and £3000 from Sarah Ann Cawston (of whom more in
a moment). This would have been rapidly depleted if we take
Miss Hill's costs as a yardstick. It is quite possible that Sam, who
would be making good money as a London solicitor, helped her
out. At any rate, when he died twenty years later, the net value
of his estate was £31,400, not a large amount for a man of his
profession at the time. Ellen inherited at most £17,000 from
him, and on her death, in 1929, her estate was valued at £28,400.
To the best of my knowledge, she never entered paid employment; so she was obviously no spendthrift.

The industrial schools that came under her responsibility
provided residential care for vagrant children aged seven to four-
teen (although some were younger); after the introduction of
compulsory education in 1870, they also housed truants. The
'industrial' in the name of these schools came from the fact that,
beside basic education, the children were taught a selection of
practical skills that would be useful to them when they grew up.
Many schools favoured the cutting of firewood by their boys, as
this could also provide a useful source of income for the school.

The most common activities, which varied from school to school, were carpentry, tailoring and shoemaking for boys; cooking, laundry work and sewing for girls. The country schools favoured gardening and farmwork, because they helped to feed and clothe the resident children. In 1898, there were some 24,000 children in industrial schools throughout the nation, most them boys. The LSB administered four residential industrial schools, two truant schools and three day industrial schools. It also sent children to sixty-four independent schools outside London. The Industrial Schools Committee reported regularly to the Board on both its own schools and on the schools to which it sent children.

Ellen also sat on the LSB sub-committee on 'schools for special instruction, for the deaf and for the blind'; in that capacity she became involved in the Passmore Edwards Settlement. The origin of this institution lies with Mary Ward, better known at the time as the novelist Mrs Humphrey Ward. Inspired by the Settlement Movement, which aimed to offer social services to the urban poor, she used her own money to open University Hall, in Gordon Square, in 1890. An appeal for more funds brought in the philanthropist Passmore Edwards, thanks to whom a purpose-designed building was erected in Tavistock Place, and named after him, one of about seventy such buildings that he financed throughout the country. Opened in 1898, it provided accommodation for the warden and eighteen resident scholars, plus classrooms, club rooms, entertainment rooms, a gymnasium, a hall seating five hundred people, and a library. Having spare rooms, Mary Ward was moved to offer them for the use of children with disabilities, if the LSB would provide the staff, and this is where Ellen came in. In collaboration with a gifted head teacher, Mrs Burgwin, she designed the equipment for the children: 'cane wheelchairs, couches, a go-kart for the playground.'[163] This became England's first school for physically impaired children; it opened in 1899. By 1903, the Board was overseeing seventy schools for mentally and physically disabled children, formed on the model of what became known as the Mary Ward Centre. But in 1904 (the year Ellen turned sixty), the London School Board was superseded by the London County Council, and women had to begin their struggle all over again.

The Education Act of 1902 did away with the 2,568 school boards set up by the Elementary Education Act of 1870 and by the same token robbed women of the right to be elected to the new Local Education Authorities. While the Act was yet a Bill, the Women's Local Government Society sent three delegates, one of whom was Ellen, to the Board of Education to register their objections. She was also in the groups of women who wrote letters of protest to *The Times* and other newspapers, to little avail. Only the passing of the Qualification of Women (County and Borough Councils) Act of 1907 finally granted them the right to be elected, and it was not until the 1910 elections that it came into effect. During this wasted decade for women's rights in local government, Ellen transferred her energies to the suffragist movement. A member of the Central Society for Women's Suffrage, she joined its executive in 1903 and became its honorary treasurer in 1906, standing down in 1909. That year she organized a debate on Women's Suffrage (in her capacity as President of the St. Pancras branch of the National Union of Women's Suffrage Societies) between Millicent Garrett Fawcett and Mary Ward (a notorious anti-suffragist) at the Passmore Edwards Settlement. At the conclusion of the debate, a straw poll was taken and, much to Mrs Ward's disgust, the figures were 74 to 235 in favour of suffrage.

᭡

One of the sources of information that I have been drawing on for Ellen's activities in London is Chapter Five of *Women, Educational Policy-Making and Administration in England*, titled "'Women not wanted": the fight to secure political representation on Local Education Authorities, 1870–1907' by Professor Jane Martin. It happens that Chapter Four of the same book, 'Women school board members and women school managers: the structuring of educational authority in Manchester and Liverpool, 1870–1903' by Professor Joyce Goodman, deals at some length with the work of Mary Dendy (1855–1933), who pioneered residential homes and hospitals in the Manchester area for what were then called 'the feeble minded,' particularly deaf children. Neither author mentions that Ellen McKee and Mary Dendy were close friends.

To learn how this came about, we have to go back to the early 1840s, when Miss J was a visitor in the home of the Beards. She and Mary Beard decided to do something for Miss J's aunt, Ruth Jeffery, at whose school near Horsham they had become friends. Ruth Jeffery was now in her mid-forties, and the school on which she depended for her livelihood was failing. Miss J and Mary persuaded her to come up to Manchester and open a school there, where the Beards could help by directing pupils to it. She came, and for a short while Mary Beard sent her eldest daughter, Sarah, to Ruth for an hour or two in the day. However, the new school was not a success,* and to supplement her income, Ruth Jeffery took in a lodger, a young man from Horsham, John Dendy (1828–94), who had come up to study at Manchester Unitarian College. (It had returned to Manchester in 1840.) His guardian, a Mr Agate, was a friend of Ruth Jeffery's; he asked her to find accommodation for the young man when he headed up north.[164]

I have already mentioned the Dendy family, putting them in parallel with the Eversheds. The two families had longstanding interconnections; after the death of John's father in 1830, his mother established yet another link by marrying a William Evershed – but she too died when John was still a teenager;

---

* After a short while, Ruth Jeffery returned south. She married a retired naval officer, Daniel Quinton, in June 1848.

hence his need for a guardian. There was also a link between John and Miss J's father: his grandfather, another John Dendy, was the minister who preceded John Jeffery at Billingshurst.

Thus Sarah Beard got to know John Dendy, fell in love and married him as soon as she was twenty-one. She believed that the education her father had given her made her 'a better mother for my children than any other training could have done.'[165] She and John were certainly very successful as parents, producing a brood of nine notable children. For lack of space, I'll mention only those (in order of birth) who have a Wikipedia page dedicated to them: John Dendy OBE; Mary Dendy MA; Helen, who married the philosopher Bernard Bosanquet; and Arthur Dendy DSC, FRS, FLS, FZS, the great zoologist. The last three feature in the following pages.

Although John Dendy trained as a Unitarian minister, he set up a silk factory with a friend soon after he graduated, and for thirty years or so they did very well, but around 1880 their firm failed – were they beaten by Courtaulds? – and Dendy reverted to his original calling, on a much reduced income. Suddenly, his unmarried daughters had to fend for themselves, and his eldest daughter Mary (1858–1933), who had been publishing stories and poetry (which did not bring in enough to live on, of course; HM was practically the only nineteenth-century woman who managed to live by her pen), sought congenial employment. Luckily, Ellen had maintained contact with the Beards and in particular with Sarah and John Dendy. When Mary spent the academic year of 1874–75 at Bedford College in London, Ellen proved as useful as her mother had ever been by introducing Mary to her cousin Sarah Wilhelmina Warren (1835–1924); she became Mary's best friend in London – and a friend for life.[166] It was also Ellen who found a job for Mary.

When Samuel Courtauld (III) died in the spring of 1881,* he

* In a curious linking with where this story began, Samuel was comforted on his deathbed by James Martineau. Samuel had met him through his

Sarah Beard and her little brother James Rait Beard, c.1848

bequeathed Folley House (with its tenant farm of seventy acres and five acres of garden) to his adopted daughter, Sarah Ann Cawston. Now in her early forties and unmarried, she found herself rattling around in the large house. Hearing of Miss Cawston's desire for a companion, Ellen proposed Mary Dendy; she arrived in June 1882, and spent seven very happy years at Folley House. Mary liked Miss Cawston immensely, for she was well educated and culturally curious, and her affection was reci-

involvement in the Unitarian Church.

procated. They would go up to London together to see Ellen, and Sarah Warren, and attend a play (Henry Irving in *Macbeth*!) or a Gilbert and Sullivan opera; they travelled to Switzerland and Italy. Together they ran the Folley House farm in place of the tenant; Mary took over the Sunday school in the village (estimated at the time of Samuel Courtauld's death to comprise all of forty cottages), wrote and produced school plays, organized a sewing class for girls and a club for older pupils and teachers.

> She checked the accounts of the Coffee House, Day School and Farm, managed the domestic staff of the House, rendered first aid to field workers in distress, and, in general, acted as bailiff or factor on the estate and as secretary or confidante of the mistress.[167]

In short, she became a pillar of the little community. She also wrote for the *Sunday School Helper* and had a novel serialized (under a pseudonym) in *All the Year Round*. This all came to an end with the sudden death of Miss Cawston in November 1889, as a result of illness contracted on the Continent.

There followed what Mary called her 'period of probation',[168] during which she travelled for her health, twice visiting her brother Arthur in Australia. Settling in Manchester, she renewed contact with her sister Sarah Louisa (notice the names), who was so outstanding a teacher at the High School for Girls in Manchester that she was awarded an honorary MA for her work.

She also caught up with her youngest sister Helen, who was working with London's Charity Organisation Society, visiting a great many poor families and observing their lives with sympathy. These experiences resulted in Helen's books, *Aspects of the Social Problem* (1895) and *Rich and Poor* (1896) – to mention only two published before the end of the century; many more were to follow – which laid the foundations for the development of social work in Britain. She married Bernard Bosanquet in 1895, and in 1905 she was appointed a member of the Royal Commission on Poor Law Methods and the Problem of Unemployment. In 1909 it produced two conflicting reports – Helen was the principal author of the majority report – which were largely ignored by the welfare reforms introduced by the Liberal government. The division of the Commission is best typified by the ideological opposition between the Fabian Socialists Sidney and Beatrice Webb, who wanted government control over everything, including funding, and Helen Bosanquet (supported by her husband), whose experience with the Charity Organisation Society inspired her view that wealthy individuals should work through charity organizations to fund support and housing for the poor (and for children with disabilities).

During this period, Mary Dendy visited countless workhouses, Cottage Homes, Model Dwellings and Industrial Schools in the Manchester area, and gave numerous talks on education, women's suffrage, and domestic economy. She also did a great deal of voluntary work in the city's clubs for children (particularly the Collyhurst Recreation Rooms, founded by her uncle James Rait Beard who, you will recall, had attended the McKees' school in Pendleton for a year). It took until 1896 – the year before Ellen was elected to the LSB – for Mary to gain a seat on the Manchester School Board. Co-opted during 1896 and 1897, she served alongside Emmeline Pankhurst on the last Board from 1900 to 1903. Visiting schools in the area, she soon realized that her calling was the care and education of children with intellectual and developmental disabilities. In 1897 she arranged to visit London, to see what was being done there. There is no record of the discussions she must have had with Ellen McKee and Helen Bosanquet on this occasion, nor (for that matter) do we know anything of meetings between Ellen and Helen, although their paths must have crossed. It was probably at this time that Mary met Millicent Garrett Fawcett, finding her 'very kind and encouraging,'[169] although no record seems to exist of their meeting; nor have I discovered any letters exchanged between Mary and the other women at this time. (Mary kept a detailed journal, from which Herbert McLachlan made many quotations in *Records of a Family*, but it has not been seen since his book was published in 1935.) That said, the very similar activities of Mary Dendy, her sister Helen, and Ellen McKee, at exactly the same time, point without a shadow of doubt to concertation between them.

Mary dedicated the rest of her life to creating and funding homes and a hospital for children with disabilities. Not surprisingly, her work was singled out by the 1904 Royal Commission as 'the most complete experiment for providing permanently for the feeble-minded,'[170] for she practised what her sister Helen preached: her institutions were almost entirely funded by private donations and charitable organizations. Ten years later, as Parliament debated the Mental Deficiency Bill, which provided for the care and management of four grades of Mental Defectives, Mary had the 'curious' experience, sitting in the Ladies' Gallery of the House, of 'hearing oneself and one's work talked about.'[171] Only three MPs voted against the Bill, which became an Act on 15 August 1913. That was the fruit of twenty years of tireless and selfless dedication – notice how, even in her private journal, Mary avoided the first person and wrote 'oneself' instead of 'myself'. After her death in 1933, the institutions she had created were named after her; in the mid-1950s, they were absorbed into the National Health Service; they were closed in 1986.

There is a romantic footnote to this tale of interlocking lives, another link in the complex web of marriages. Mary Dendy's brother Arthur, ten years her junior, much enjoyed visiting Folley House and taking Mary on trips up to London. At the end of 1887, having made a name for himself as a promising young zoologist, he was invited to take up a post at the University of Melbourne. Before leaving, he spent Christmas with Mary and Miss Cawston at Folley House. Also staying there was Ada

Margaret Courtauld, a great niece of Miss J's uncle, Samuel Courtauld (III). On the evening of 1 January 1888, she and Arthur went ice skating together by the light of a lantern. By 12 January, they had come to an understanding. A few days later, he sailed for Australia; she followed him, without undue haste, arriving on 6 November; they married on 4 December 1888.* Over the next few years, they had three daughters and a son.[172] When Mary visited them, they surely harked back to that Christmas at Folley House with Miss Cawston.

E<small>LLEN</small> M<small>C</small>K<small>EE</small> DIED ON 2 September 1929, leaving half her residual estate to Mary Dendy. Her adult life had spanned quite precisely the great period of the struggle for women's rights, from the Petition of 1866 (when she was almost twenty-one) to the Representation of the People (Equal Franchise) Act of 1928, which gave the vote to *all* women over twenty-one, regardless of property ownership.

This remarkable story of networking women really began when the orphan Miss J made friends with Mary Barnes at her aunt Ruth's school. After Mary married John Relly Beard, Miss J became as close to their family as she could have been without actually marrying into it. Instead, she married Beard's assistant, and gave birth to Ellen McKee. Beard's ideas on the education of women made a lasting impression. Soon after this, Miss J's cousin Mentia Taylor began to campaign for women's rights.

* In her Will, Sarah Ann Cawston left Ada Margaret Courtauld £1500.

Another thread began when Miss J became the deaf Harriet Martineau's travel companion – and then lifelong friend. Over the years, starting from the 1820s, HM had variously advocated equality between men and women in their education, in their pay, and in marriage. She also pointed to the number of children with learning difficulties caused by impaired hearing, speech and sight, and demanded that they be enabled to live useful and fulfilling lives just like other people. Miss J accompanied HM on her visits to schools and homes for blind, deaf and dumb children in America. HM herself demonstrated that deafness need not be an obstacle to clarity of thought and expression.

These two threads merged in Ellen's life, the direction of which was influenced by Harriet Martineau and then Mentia Taylor. Having campaigned for the right of women to participate in local government, she was elected to the London School Board at exactly the same time that her friend Mary Dendy, John Relly Beard's granddaughter, began to serve on the Manchester School Board. They each in their own way pioneered in providing dedicated facilties for physically disabled children, a social service that is now the norm in all civilized countries.

These innovations were empowered by the exceptional intelligence of Harriet Martineau and her courageous defiance of convention: she spoke up openly and frankly. That ruined her reputation, but she rendered an immense service to 'the other half of the human race' and to all those who were disadvantaged, if not by their gender, then by physical impairments like her own.

Acknowledgements

The photograph of Folley House (p.32) is from volume two of the *Courtauld Family Letters,* and the double portrait of Sarah and James Rait Beard (p.73) is from McLachlan, *Records of a Family.* The source of the picture on page 37 is provided in the caption, in the Note to this edition (p.vi), and in the list of sources as well.

Harriet Martineau's previously unpublished letter to Miss J that accompanied the MS of *Society in America* is quoted (on p.44) courtesy of the Morgan Library and Museum, New York. Ellen McKee sold the MS to the Library in 1910 (for the sum of £150, roughly $750 at the time), along with its accompanying four-page letter. The Library's accession number for this item is MA 873.1. My grateful thanks to Christine Nelson for her help with this.

Amy Miller, Assistant Librarian and Archivist in the Research Library of the Buffalo History Museum, provided me with a copy of HM's letter which is quoted from *Studies of the Niagara Frontier* by Frank H. Severance on pages 35 and 37.

Elizabeth Crawford (whose reference guide to the suffrage movement was my first source of information about the lives of Miss J and Ellen McKee) helped me with the 1851 census entry for Blendon Hall, and pointed out a mistake in my bibliography.

Jeff Watson provided detailed information about the Jeffery family and the Rev. John Jeffery's brewery.

Margaret Macilwain, author of *Mentia: Mrs Peter Taylor (1810–1908) a radical liberal Victorian, 'the mother' of the English women's parliamentary suffrage movement* (2018), generously commented on my references to Mentia, told me of the link between John Jeffery's niece and the Eversheds, and also spotted some typos.

Gillian Murphy at the Women's Library Collection at the LSE Library, London, very kindly copied two letters (that I have not quoted from) for me.

The John Rylands Library at the University of Manchester provided copies of letters to Miss J from HM's relatives. They are in the Unitarian College Collection, which is formed around John Relly Beard and his descendants.

Béatrice Bourgeois, of the Lausanne University Library, patiently mediated the inter-library loan of the various books that I requested.

My friend and fellow writer, Laurence Bristow-Smith, commented frankly on a draft of this monograph and pointed to passages that I could express more clearly.

I should also like to express my warm thanks to all those who generously – but ultimately unsuccessfully – attempted to help with the research that this investigation entailed: Stuart Coupe (the Lay Person in charge of the chapel at Billingshurst); Bill Evershed, Susie Evershed, and Duncan Rabagliati (who put me in contact with Jeff Watson); Imogen Russell (searchroom assistant at the West Sussex Record Office); the Rev. Emma Walsh (College Librarian) and Emily Burgoyne (the Angus Librarian) at Regent's Park College, Oxford; and Jan Wood, Archivist at the Devon Heritage Centre (Devon Archives and Local Studies Service).

Sources

Bartlett, W. H. *American Scenery, or Land, Lake, and River. Illustrations of Transatlantic Nature from Drawings by N[athaniel] P[arker] Willis.* 2 volumes. London: George Virtue, 1840.

Burkhardt, Frederick, and Sydney Smith, eds, *The Correspondence of Charles Darwin*, Vol.1., 1821–36. Cambridge: CUP, 1985.

Carpenter, J. Estlin. *James Martineau: Theologian and Teacher. A Study of his Life and Thought.* London: Philip Green, 1905.

Chapman, Maria Weston, *Memorials of Harriet Martineau.* Ed. Deborah Anna Logan. Bethlehem: Lehigh University Press, 2015.

Cherry-Garrard, Apsley. *The Worst Journey in the World. With Scott in Antarctica 1910–1913.* Mineola, New York: Dover, 2010.

Coleman, D. C. *Courtaulds: an Economic and Social History.* 3 vols. Oxford: OUP, 1969.

Courtauld Family Letters: 1782–1900. 8 volumes. Cambridge: Bowes & Bowes, 1916.

Courtauld, S[tephen] L. (ed.). *The Huguenot Family of Courtauld.* 3 vols. Privately printed, 1957–67.

Courtney, Janet Elizabeth Hogarth. *Freethinkers of the Nineteenth Century.* London, Chapman & Hall, 1920.

Crawford, Elizabeth. *The Women's Suffrage Movement: A Reference Guide, 1866–1928.* UCL Press, 1998.

Davidoff, Leonore. *Thicker than Water: Siblings and Their Relations, 1780–1920.* Oxford: OUP, 2012.

Gear, Gillian Carol. *Industrial Schools In England, 1857–1933: 'Moral Hospitals,' or 'Oppressive Institutions'?* PhD thesis, University of London Institute of Education, 1999.

Gooday, Graeme, and Karen Sayer. *Managing the Experience of Hearing Loss in Britain, 1830–1930.* London: Palgrave, 2017.

Hill, Michael R. 'A Methodological Comparison of Harriet Martineau's *Society in America* (1837) and Alexis de Tocqueville's *Democracy in America* (1835–1840).' In *Harriet Martineau: Theoretical and Methodological Perspectives*, ed. Michael R. Hill and Susan Hoecker-Drysdale. New York: Routledge, 2001, pp.59–74.

Hollis, Patricia, *Ladies Elect: Women in English Local Government 1865–1914.* London & New York: Clarendon Press, Oxford University Press, 1987.

Logan, Deborah Anna, ed. *The Collected Letters of Harriet Martineau.* 5 volumes. London: Pickering & Chatto, 2007.

McLachlan, H. *Records of a Family 1800–1933: Pioneers in Education, Social Service and Liberal Religion.* Manchester: Manchester U P, 1933.

Martin, Jane. *The role of women in education of the working classes: 1870–1904.* Open University PhD thesis, 1991.

——— *Women and the Politics of Schooling in Victorian and Edwardian England.* London & New York: Leicester U P, 1998.

——— '"Women not wanted": The fight to secure political representation on Local Education Authorities, 1870–1907', chapter 5 of *Women, Educational Policy-Making and Administration in England,* edited by Joyce Goodman, Sylvia Harrop. London & New York: Routledge, 2000.

Martineau, Harriet. *Autobiography.* Ed. Maria Weston Chapman. Boston: James R. Osgood & Co, 1877.

——— *Autobiography.* Ed. Linda H. Peterson. Peterborough, Ont., Canada: Broadview Press, 2007.

——— *Further Letters.* Ed. Deborah A. Logan. Bethlehem: Lehigh U P, 2012.

——— *How to Observe Morals and Manners.* London: Knight, 1838.

——— *Letters on Mesmerism.* London: E. Moxon, 1845.

Martineau, Harriet. *Retrospect of Western Travel.* 3 vols. London: Saunders & Otley, 1838.

——— *Society in America.* 2 vols. London: Saunders and Otley, 1837.

Miller, Fenwick. *Harriet Martineau.* Boston: Roberts Bros, 1887.

Murray, Janet Horowitz and Myra Stark, eds. *The Englishwoman's Review of Social and Industrial Questions: 1899.* Routledge Library edition.

Ryall, Anka. 'Medical Body and Lived Experience: the case of Harriet Martineau.' *Mosaic*, Vol. 33, No.4, 2000, pp.35–53.

Severance, Frank H. *Studies of the Niagara Frontier.* Buffalo Historical Society Publications, Vol. 15. Buffalo, New York, 1911.

Solly, Henry. *'These Eighty Years': Or, The Story of an Unfinished Life.* London, 1893.

Styler, Rebecca. *Religion, Gender, Genre: Nineteenth-Century Women's Theology.* Ph D thesis, University of Leicester. 2005.

Taylor, Peter Alfred, comp. and ed. *Some Account of the Family of Taylor (formerly Taylard).* One hundred copies printed for private circulation, London, 1875.

Townsend, Ben. *Providence Chapel – the last survival of Horsham Barracks.* 2016. https://www.providencechapelcharlwood.org/resources/Military%20research%20%26%20history.pdf

Source Notes

In these notes, books and articles are identified by the writer's surname, works by HM by their title alone, and the titles of collections of her letters are shortened to:

Memorials for Maria Chapman, *Memorials of Harriet Martineau* (ed. Deborah Logan); and

Collected Letters for *The Collected Letters of Harriet Martineau* (ed. Deborah Logan).

1 As reported by Fenwick Miller, Chapter 4.
2 *Autobiography*, Vol. 1, p.329.
3 *Autobiography*, Vol. 1, p.462.
4 Courtney, p.199.
5 Darwin Correspondence Project, 'Letter no. 321,' accessed on 10 March 2019, http://www.darwinproject.ac.uk/DCP-LETT-321
6 *The Mill on the Floss*, Book I, ch. 2.
7 *Autobiography*, Vol. 1, p.179.
8 *Autobiography*, Vol. 1, pp.122–3.
9 *Autobiography*, Vol. 1, p.330.
10 *Autobiography*, Vol. 1, p.108.
8 Quoted by Cherry-Garrard. p.549.
9 *Society in America*, Vol. I, p.v.
10 Letter to William Tait, dated 29 August 1833, *Collected Letters*, Vol. 1, p.213. HM's emphasis.
11 *How to Observe*, part II, 'What to Observe.' The emphases are HM's.
15 *Autobiography*, Vol. 1, p.331.
16 McLachlan, p.7.
17 *Autobiography* (ed. Peterson), p.331, note 2.
18 I published a brief outline, 'What We Know of Miss J' in *Notes and Queries*, Volume 65, Issue 3, 1 September 2018, pp.365–8.
19 4 November 1782. Wiston/3334 West Sussex Record Office.
20 From the obituary by J.B. printed in the *Monthly Repository*, 1815, p.524.

21 Information from advertisements in the *Sussex Advertiser*, kindly supplied by Jeff Watson.
22 *Monthly Magazine*, 1805, p.371.
23 Letter dated 14 December, 1816, from George Courtauld (I) to his daughter Sophia. *Courtauld Family Letters*, Vol. 1, pp.223–4.
24 *Atheneum*, 1808, p.205.
25 Taylor, p.618.
26 Taylor, p.653.
27 Letter dated 10 February 1814, *Courtauld Family Letters*, Vol. 1, p.100.
28 Letter dated 23 October 1814, *Courtauld Family Letters*, Vol. 1, p.107.
29 Letter dated 23 March 1816, *Courtauld Family Letters*, Vol. 1, p.192.
30 Letter dated 30 May 1815, *Courtauld Family Letters*, Vol. 1, p.121.
31 Obituary in the *Monthly Repository*, 1815, p.524.
32 Letter dated 18 May 1815 from Mrs Ruth Courtauld to her son George at Billingshurst, *Courtauld Family Letters*, Vol. 1, p.18.
33 Letter from the winter of 1814/15 from Louisa Perina Courtauld to her brother George at Billingshurst, *Courtauld Family Letters*, Vol. 1, p.149.
34 Letter dated 15 June 1815 from Kate Courtauld to her sister Sophia, *Courtauld Family Letters*, Vol. 1, p.137.
35 Letter dated 18 May 1815, *Courtauld Family Letters*, Vol. 1, p.118.
36 This is confirmed in a letter from Kate to her sister Sophia dated 21 June 1815, *Courtauld Family Letters*, Vol. 1, pp.138–9.
37 McLachlan, p.111.
38 Letter dated 4 January 1815, *Courtauld Family Letters*, Vol. 1, p.110. I believe that, writing early in the new year, George Courtauld forgot it was already 1816. Internal evidence supports this.
39 Letter dated 29 January 1816, *Courtauld Family Letters*, Vol. 1, p.173.
40 Letter dated 5 February 1816 from Mrs Ruth Courtauld to her son George, *Courtauld Family Letters*, Vol. 1, p.176.
41 Letter dated 2 March 1816 from Kate Courtauld to her brother George, *Courtauld Family Letters*, Vol. 1, p 188.
42 *Courtauld Family Letters*, Vol. 8, p.3571.
43 *The Huguenot Family of Courtauld*, Vol. 2, p.14.
44 *Courtauld Family Letters*, Vol. 1, p.xiii.
45 Letter from George Courtauld (I) to his sisters, *Courtauld Family Letters*, Vol. 2, p.742.
46 Letter dated 21 February 1818 from George Courtauld to his daughter Sophia, *Courtauld Family Letters*, Vol. 2, p.352.
47 Letter from Mrs Taylor dated 3 June 1823, *Courtauld Family Letters*, Vol. 3, p.1039.

48   *Huguenot Family of Courtauld,* Vol.2, p.86.
49   Letter dated 6 January 1824 from Christiana Lambert to Sophia
      Courtauld, *Courtauld Family Letters,* Vol. 3, p.1146.
50   Taylor, p.591.
51   Letter dated 12 October 1826 from Samuel Courtauld (III) to his sister
      Sophy, *Courtauld Family Letters,* Vol. 4, p.1509.
52   Letter dated 4 March 1827 from Christiana Lambert to Sophia Courtauld,
      Courtauld Family Letters, Vol. 4, p.1541.
53   Letter dated 23 July 1827 from Christiana Lambert to Sophia Courtauld,
      Courtauld Family Letters, Vol. 4, p.1558.
54   From the *Law Times,* Vol. 32.
55   Letter dated 9 August 1837 from Kate (Mrs P. A.) Taylor to Sophia
      Courtauld, *Courtauld Family Letters,* Vol. 6, p.2647.
56   Taylor, p.506.
57   Taylor, p.507.
58   Taylor, p.507
59   Letter dated 13 December 1830 from Maria Minton to Sophia Courtauld,
      Courtauld Family Letters, Vol. 4, p.1808.
60   Letter of 24 April 1833 from Kate (Mrs P. A.) Taylor to her sister Sophia,
      Courtauld Family Letters, Vol. 5, p.2106.
61   Letter of 28 May 1833 from Kate (Mrs P. A.) Taylor to her sister Sophia,
      Courtauld Family Letters, Vol. 5, p.2119.
62   Letter of 8 July 1833 from Maria Minton to Sophia Courtauld, *Courtauld
      Family Letters,* Vol. 5, p.2139.
63   Letter of July 1833 (no day) from Maria Minton to Sophia Courtauld,
      Courtauld Family Letters, Vol. 5, p.2142.
64   *Collected Letters,* Vol.I, p.225.
65   Letter dated 10 February 1834 to Ezra Stiles Gannett, *Collected Letters,*
      Vol. I, p.236.
66   Carpenter, pp.8 and 38.
67   McLachlan, p.34.
68   McLachlan, p.13.
69   *Further Letters,* p.449
70   Styler, pp.82–3.
71   Letter quoted by McLachlan, p.26. Not included in any collection of
      HM's letters.
72   Letter from Samuel Courtauld to his sister Sophia, *Courtauld Family
      Letters,* Vol. 5, p.2035.
73   Letter dated March 1835 from Kate (Mrs P.A.) Taylor to Sophia,
      Courtauld Family Letters, Vol. 5, p.2325.

74 *Courtauld Family Letters,* Vol. 7, p.3142.
75 Letter postmarked 11 August 1848 to Sophia, *Courtauld Family Letters,* Vol. 7, p.3318.
76 Letter dated 27 September 1833 [sic for 32] from Isabella Bell to Sophia Courtauld, *Courtauld Family Letters,* Vol. 5, p.2023.
77 *Autobiography,* Vol.1, p.331.
78 *The Importance of Being Earnest,* Act III.
79 *Collected Letters,* Vol.1, p.225.
80 *Collected Letters,* Vol.1, p.246.
81 *Collected Letters,* Vol.1, p.254.
82 Letter dated 26 February 1835 from Kate (Mrs P.A.) Taylor to Sophia, *Courtauld Family Letters,* Vol. 6, p.2322.
84 Letter dated 30 July 1835 from Louisa Perina Courtauld to Sophia and Kate (Mrs P.A.) Taylor, *Courtauld Family Letters,* Vol. 6, pp.2412–13.
84 Severance, p.285.
85 *Courtauld Family Letters,* Vol.6.
86 *Autobiography,* Vol.1, p.353.
87 *Collected Letters,* Vol.1, pp.208–209.
88 Severance, p.287.
89 *Retrospect of Western Travel,* p.162.
90 *Autobiography,* pp.394-5.
91 *Autobiography,* Vol.1, p.336.
92 *Autobiography,* Vol.1, p.341.
93 *Autobiography,* Vol.1, p.370.
94 *Autobiography,* Vol.1, p.348.
95 *Autobiography,* Vol.1, p.351.
96 *Autobiography,* Vol.1, p.369.
97 *Autobiography,* Vol.1, p.369.
98 *Autobiography,* Vol.1, p.364.
99 *Autobiography,* Vol.1, p.332.
100 *Collected Letters,* Vol 1, p.290.
101 *Autobiography,* Vol.1, p.371.
102 Letter dated 30 November 1836 from Sarah Bromley to Sophia, *Courtauld Family Letters,* Vol. 6, p.2576. The emphases are hers.
103 Letter dated 22 July 1837 from Sarah Bromley to Sophia, *Courtauld Family Letters,* Vol. 6, p.2624.
104 Letter dated 9 August 1837 from Kate (Mrs P. A.) Taylor to Sophia, *Courtauld Family Letters,* Vol. 6, p.2631.
105 Letter dated 9 August 1837 from Kate (Mrs P. A.) Taylor to Sophia, *Courtauld Family Letters,* Vol. 6, p.2647.

106 *Collected Letters*, Vol. 2, p.25.
107 Ryall, p.38.
108 Chapman, p.443.
109 Chapman, p.443-4.
110 McLachlan, p.111.
111 McLachlan, p.8.
112 McLachlan, p.118.
113 McLachlan, p.6.
114 McLachlan, p.115.
115 Letter dated 11 October 1842, Chapman, p.444.
116 Chapman, p.446.
117 Chapman, p.446-7.
118 *The Gentleman's Magazine*. Vol. 175, 1844, p.196.
119 Solly, vol.1, p.403.
120 McLachlan, p.36.
121 McLachlan, pp.104-27.
122 Letter dated 24 January 1844 from Georgiana Bell to Sophia, *Courtauld Family Letters*, Vol. 6, p.3012.
123 Letter from HM to Sophia, *Courtauld Family Letters*, Vol 7, pp. 3326. Not included in any collection of HM's letters.
124 Mentioned in a letter dated 2 March 1846 from Mrs P.A.Taylor to Sophia, *Courtauld Family Letters*, Vol 7, p.3131.
125 Letter dated March 1846 from HM to Louisa McKee, *Courtauld Family Letters*, Vol 7, pp. 3136-7. Not included in any collection of HM's letters.
126 Letter dated 13 June 1846 from Samuel Courtauld to his brother George, *Courtauld Family Letters*, Vol 7, p.3144.
127 Letter dated April 1846 from HM to Sophia Courtauld, *Courtauld Family Letters*, Vol 7, p.3138-9. Not included in any collection of HM's letters.
128 Letter dated 9 June, 1848, from HM to Sophia, *Courtauld Family Letters*, Vol 7, p.3318. Not included in any collection of HM's letters.
129 Letter dated September 1848. *Courtauld Family Letters*, Vol 7, p.3326.
130 *Collected Letters*, Vol. 3, p.38.
131 Letter dated 5 August 1847 from HM to Sophia Courtauld, *Courtauld Family Letters*, Vol 7, p.3247. Not included in any collection of HM's letters.
132 Martin, p.91.
133 *Collected Letters*, Vol. 3, p.63.
134 Chapman, p.466.
135 Chapman, p.454.
136 *Autobiography*, p.332.

137 Chapman, p.443; HM's emphasis.
138 Chapman, p.475.
139 Chapman, p.471.
140 Chapman, p.472; HM's emphasis.
141 Chapman, p.469; HM's emphasis.
142 Chapman, p.456; my emphasis.
131 March 1854, Chapman, p.466.
144 Chapman, p.464.
145 Courtney, p.263.
146 *Autobiography,* p.151.
147 *The Dictionary of National Biography*, quoted from Wikisource.
148 Chapman, p.487.
149 Chapman, p.487.
150 Chapman, p.488. Letter dated 21 March 1875.
151 Chapman, p.490. Letter dated 28 April 1875.
152 Chapman, p.492, HM's emphasis.
153 Chapman, p.493.
154 Information from Martin (1991), p.278.
155 *The Times,* 29 November 1870, quoted by Hollis, p.72.
156 Hollis, p.vii.
157 *The Englishwoman's Review.*
158 Martin (2000), p.80; my emphasis.
159 Hollis, p.101.
160 Hollis, p.102.
161 Hollis, p.101.
162 Martin (1998), p.88.
163 Hollis, p.125.
164 I owe most of the information in this paragraph to McLachlan, mainly p.111.
165 McLachlan, p.111.
166 McLachlan, p.141.
167 McLachlan, p138.
168 McLachlan, p.147.
169 McLachlan, p.145.
170 Part V of the *Report*, quoted by McLachlan, p.169.
171 McLachlan, p.173.
172 I owe this information, and much more about Mary and Arthur Dendy, to McLachlan, Chapters 8 and 10.

www.ingramcontent.com/pod-product-compliance
Lightning Source LLC
Chambersburg PA
CBHW020328130626
46549CB00003B/1078